Secular Thoughts of the SIKH GURUS

Dr. Vivek Ranjan Bhattacharya
M.A., Ph.D.

Foreword by

Giani Zail Singh

Gian Publishing House
Delhi-110007

Gian Publishing House
29/6, Shakti Nagar
Delhi-110007

ISBN 81-212-0231-0

Printed in India

Published by Mrs Gayatri Garg for Gian Publishing House, Delhi-110007, Typeset & Designed at DTP Services & Consultancy (P) Ltd., Delhi and Printed at Goyal Offset Printers, Delhi.

To

*Justice **Ranjit Singh Sarkaria***
A true Indian
and a
sincere Sikh
on his deep learning and
dedication to
Indian culture

FOREWORD

The basic concept of the Sikh Gurus is the universality of Almighty God and the brotherhood of man. The Supreme being is omnipotent, omniscient and omnipresent. He is omniform, unborn and the Creator. He is the saviour, benefactor, kind and just. The Gurus exhorted mankind to sing the glory of the fearless, the Ocean of Mercy, the Fountain of all comfort and source of all wisdom. All gifts are given by Him. He pervades all places, all hearts, all homes and hearths. His treasures are inexhaustible. His Name is the priceless jewel and His power, His Grace, His healing power is for every one.

The Sikh Gurus also taught mankind that the soul is immortal; this physical form is the result of one's actions. All one's actions without remembering Him are futile as decorations on a dead body. Man will have to render an account of his deeds. Life devoid of goodness is all in vain. Futile are distinctions based on caste and pedigree. Any one having conceit of his caste is ignorant of His ways.

Guru Nanak the first in the lineage of Ten Masters said that he would go with the lowliest of the low, as he does not know of any difference in men on the basis of caste or birth. The rich and the poor are all brethren. Guru Nanak advocated renunciation of luxury, anger and lust, but not of one's kith and kin. Instead of escaping to the forests and loneliness, one should lead a normal life of worldiness with one's family and exist like a lotus that stands above its roots which are in mud.

Guru Nank was born in 1469 AD at a time when India was in utter confusion and crisis. Babar's invasion had created a turmoil and accompanied by atrocities of caste system coupled with social injustice, the people were caught in a web of cruelty and chaos. It was then that this great seer, a tremendous spiritual force tried to put balm on the wounds of a bruised humanity with his divine message of love and compassion. He tried to extricate humanity from the morass of parochialism and superstition.

He travelled far and wide in the company of Bala, a Hindu, and Mardana, a Muslim, to spread his teachings of universal love, tolerance, amity and social justice. Guru Nanak and the other Sikh Gurus emphasised the virtues of hard work, honest living, simple and quiet life, sympathy for the needy and the poor and contentment. Greed, avarice and high-handedness are the sins difficult to wash.

The Sikh Gurus in their divine utterance have repeatedly mentioned the Vedas and other ancient scriptures. Many times in the Adi Granth have the names of Vishnu, Brahma, Shiv, Rama, Krishna and other gods and goddesses been included in the Gurubani.

Apart from six of the ten Gurus, the utterances of nineteen non-Sikh saints and many Bhatts form part of the Holy scripture. Notable among these are Kabir, Namdev, Ravidas, Farid, Surdas, Jaidev, Dhanna and Bhikhan. It is a universal Book of Divinity in the true meaning of the word. Dr. Vivek Ranjan Bhattacharya in his brilliant work has thrown great light on the works of Guru Nanak and the other Gurus. He does not forget to mention the contribution of non-Sikh saints of India and Islamic sects. He also feels that the teachings of Guru Nanak had their influence on the writings of poet Rabindranath Tagore.

I have known Dr. Bhattacharya for over a decade and his dedication to the Indian religious thought and culture is really remarkable. He has tried to bring out in his book the spirit and the ethos of the Sikh Gurus and their impact on humanity.

The Gurus taught devotion to noble ideals of truth and sacrifice. The fifth and the ninth Gurus gave supreme sacrifice for maintaining high values of the freedom of conscience and the right of every one to profess his own faith. The tenth Guru sacrificed all his four sons and his mother in the righteous cause of justice and equity. He created Khalsa for the significant purpose of obliterating all distinctions of caste and narrow loyalties and to eradicate fear of the unjust and the cruel.

This new order was meant to preserve the best of human qualities for the service and protection of the poor and never to raise hand on the defenceless and the weak. Women were given an exalted place in society and the so-called low classes were raised to equality.

Dr. Bhattacharya has taken pains to explain the institutions of Panj Pyaras, the five Beloveds created by the tenth Guru, and the concept of five Ks, the symbols of every Sikh. I am sure the book will help spreading the message of fraternity and secularism, love and humanity, peace and brotherhood, service and sacrifice.

Much has been written on Sikh religious thought but I feel that few have highlighted the secular and immortal message of the Sikh Gurus in a manner in which Dr Vivek Rajan Bhattacharya has done. I congratulate the author for his commendable effort.

Zail Singh

(ZAIL SINGH)

4, Circular Road
Chanakya Puri
New Delhi - 110021

Introduction

To attempt a treatise on the holy works of the great Sikh Gurus is very much like measuring the depth of the ocean by a boatman's rudder! It is beyond common man's comprehension. Only a person completely dedicated to the Infinite can relish the sublime thoughts of these divine personalities. And such persons would not come to preach or describe their experiences and share their ecstatic joy to the public, because they shun publicity and want to enjoy seclusion.

But it is equally necessary to bring at least glimpses of the great spiritual experiments and experiences of such great Saints to the doorsteps of the public, because they need spiritual awakening. It is all the more necessary in a multi-religious nation, where mutual understanding stands on basic concepts of the religious teachings and preachings of such great dedicated preceptors. The author owes a personal commitment. His first five years, the pleasant days with thousands of brethren in the *Gurdwaras* at Rawalpindi has left an impression that will sustain him to have greater faith in the Gurus than anything else.

I was dedicated to the Guru by my mother, who hailed from Nanakganj, Sipri Bazaar, Jhansi, and who could attend the prayers in Gurdwaras from her childhood. I do not know whether it is still there. On *Guru Parabs* there used to be huge processions there with not only well-dressed band players, but with beautifully decorated elephants and the *Panj Payaras* being carried on them. Or it might have been the sacred *Granth Sahibji*, which used to be carried on the decorated elephants.

In Rawalpindi, being the only Bengali Sikh, I got most affectionate VIP treatment. I would attend the prayer every day. The devotees would wait for me. I would enjoy their hospitality from lap to lap. I had all the five K's. As it was difficult for a child to handle a heavy *chimta* (the musical instrument), a specially made small one was supplied to me. Even the musical Guru, who would lead the choir, the *Guru Vani,* would get me a seat next to him. There was no microphone there. I do not remember to have missed the *Shabad Kirtan* even for a day.

With the kind and affectionate touch of the brothers of the faith so deeply ingrained in my whole career, it really sometimes deeply hurts me, when I find some motivated criticism of the faith. I must confess in public, I am proud of being a Sikh in the early formative stage of my life. My father, who followed Sri Ramakrishna Paramahansa and believed equally in all the religious faiths, called me by the Sikh name till his last day. The name was Situ Singh. Even now some old Bengali Military Officers from Rawalpindi call me only by the Sikh name. It has sweet memories echoing the sounds of music by the religious *Gianis,* many of whom must have left the world by now.

The world is a temporary stage of a short life's drama. We foolish people do not know how to make best use of it. There is even limited time to enjoy such a great opportunity as that of a human being. That by itself is a great blessing of God. So when I hear any voice being raised against such a great group, it touches quickly my sensitive mind. I feel deeply hurt. If some few misled urchins make noise somewhere, the mud-sling should not be ascribed to a whole group.

The contribution of the Sikhs in the mainstream of the socio-economic-cultural life has been unique. The Sikhs are the most hard-working people in the world. For a mere eking out a living, they have spread themselves all over the world. They are deeply religious and patriotic. Shaheed Bhagat Singh apart, who does not know that the Indian National Army (INA) was started by General Mohan Singh before it was handed over to Netaji Subhas Chandra Bose? Who does not know the contribution of Punjab Kesari Lala Lajpat Rai? His mother was a Sikh lady. It is not the proper forum to discuss the role of Sikhs in our freedom movement. That by itself needs a detailed study in depth. The role of Sikhs in the freedom struggle would, I am sure, be written by some scholar one day in letters of gold.

The message of the Sikhs should not be restricted only in the *gurdwaras* and only to the Sikhs. Nanak Devji belongs to the whole world. He was a humanist among the humanists. In fact he opposed any sort of groupism like Hinduism or Islam and in his famous sermons in Mecca, he very boldly proclaimed that. It is indeed not an ordinary matter of conviction and a sign of progressiveness -that too as early as five hundred years ago - to talk so clearly about humanism as distinguished from any restricted faith - be it Hinduism or Islam. He opposed both. They had been clearly expressed in various songs so spontaneously composed by him.

The greatest contribution of Guru Nanak Devji is perhaps the transmission of the message of self-reliance. One must stand on one's own legs. Says Nank,

If a Saint or a seer goes abegging,
Go not near him, nor fall at his feet;
The one who earns his own living
And part thereof offers as charity;
He alone knows the secret of the *Panth*.

Everything materialistic in this World is of temporal value. They are necessary at certain point, but they certainly are not *summam bonum* of life. Says the Great Guru, the only thing that is significant, meaningful and key to God - realisation is *Nam*, the recitation of the Holy Name of God. Guru Nanak says, without the wealth of *Nam*, all else is futile. Attachment, ego, pride, they burn you all. True wealth through Guru's grace alone is gained. Coming and going, worldly wealth is like the shade of a tree. The wealth of the world leads to the untold miserises. Neither can it be accumulated, nor can it accompany you beyond".

Very much like the Christ, who used to say, "I and the Father are one." Guru Nanak Said,

By churning the ocean of the body, a marvel have I beheld:
Guru is God and Betwixt them there is no difference!

So Guru Nanak emphasised on the role of the Guru, non-attachment to worldly things, and immortality. In the words of Nanak Devji, "Those who have destroyed self-will and live in humility are happy. The haughty great are consumed, O, Nanak, as in a furance, by the fire of their pride".

Said Guru Nanak, "By Guru's grace gettest thou everything; so do thou serve and trust the Guru and to him sacrifice thyself hundreds of times."

Nanak Devji says, "For wealth many are ruined; this wealth hath disgraced many; It is not amassed without sin - and it accompanieth not the dead".

This great thought of renunciation was carried further by the most important of the Sikh Gurus - Guru Gobind Singhji about whom there was an erroneous idea that he had the ambition of building up an empire. Far from it, whatever he did was to protect the Sikhs from the onslaught of the Mughals especially Aurangazeb. Otherwise, he too was a great saint, whose only conception of God realisation was through renunciation.

Guru Gobind Singh himself writes,

> Emperors before whom stray-armed kings did meekly bow
> their heads in countless numbers;
> Who possessed great elephants with golden trapping, proud
> and painted with brilliant colours;
> Millions of horses swifter than the wind
> which bounded over the World;
> What mattered it how mighty were these emperors;
> All at the last went hence with nothing bare of foot.

The most intellectual poet among the Gurus, Arjan Dev Guruji said,

> Among all men that man is foremost, who in the company of saints destroys his self-attachments. He who dethrones himself the lowliest of the low, shall be deemed the highest.

All the Guru's voices sound like an echo of the highest thoughts of the *Vedanta* as popularised by Bhagavan Sankaracharya who time and again cautioned mankind from mere materialistic gains. Nanak Devji, for instance, very frequently repeated that the wealth of the World leads man to untold miseries. A true devotee does not want anything except God. Guru Ram Das said,

> Mankind runs after salvation, heaven, ceaseless is its yearning; and paradises,
> But lovers of the Lord ask not even for salvation;
> They are satisfied with His presence only.

All the Gurus were against material gains. Guru Amar Das said, man lives like a hyporcrite, the victim of his own acts; worries destroyed by worldly attachments".

Complete surrender to God and the Guru had been prescribed by all the ten Gurus. "When a man is in dire straits, and there comes none to help him, when he has lost all hope and help; let him only set his mind on the Lord;" and the Guru assures "no harm shall (ever) touch him".

For this constant thinking of the Lord is an essential pre-requisite. Says Guru Ram Das, "constant devotion alone can win his love. Like a *chatak* (rain bird) that prays for rain, we should beg for a drop of Nectar." It is quite in line with the thoughts of the Great Nanak who said "Be thou the slave of the slaves of the Master, who hath deep devotion to the Love".

One must subdue one's self-identity; One must surrender one's ego and only then he will be getting the mercy of the Guru. Guru Nanak says only he gets God-realisation "who has subdued his own self, who harms no living thing and overflows with compassion".

Guru Arjan says, "All earthly joys are of a fading colour; they pass, they become dust. But Nectar is drunk by those whom the name of God inspires."

All the Gurus preached the spirit of renunciation equally emphatically. Said Guru Nanak,

> Thou buriest endless wealth in the earth yet they desire it departeth not;
>
> They who depart desiring endless wealth shall be the Endless Treason.

In the same tune, Guru Arjan says, "The hunger for worldly wealth is never satisfied; the world's thirst is not quenched, but let a man detach himself from worldly attachments and after this trial he shall prosper".

Similarly, Guru Teg Bahadur says, "Day and night mortals search and search for wealth; Among millions few there be who remember God". This is exactly what Bhagwan Sri Ramakrishna Deva used to say every day at Daksineswar.

One must remember, warns Guru Nanak, "The mind is not aware and is enslaved by its own properties". So one has to cultivate a spiritual pursuit rigorously and regularly. That is possible only by taking refuge at the feet of the Guru:

> They are the real devotees who know God turn not away from Him;
> They who perform no service for Him are false, and slink away.

Guru Nanak clearly assured that he who is really dedicated is fearless. "He is a true disciple who is without hope or fear, he who has no fear of death is a disciple perfectly harmonized".

Talking of renunciation Guru Teg Bahadur observed, "That man who in the midst of grief is free from grinning; and free from fear and free from the snare; of delight, nor is covetous of gold that he knows to be dust; in such a man God dwelleth"..

Attachment is a great hurdle to God-realisation. Guru Arjan says, "when a man finds himself to worldly attachments, he is caught up in the endless cycle of deaths and filths. But when are his worldly delusions dissipated, he attains to oneness with God". The same saint poet says,

> "Though Thou art like a guest for the night
> Who must part betimes in the morning
> Thou makest busy thyself with the world's affairs;
> Remember this is a garden of flowers that must fade".

Highest emphasis was laid by the Gurus on character building. Guru Arjan Das says, "Those who, improve within, seem outwardly pure, fair without and foul within, have gambled their live away; they have contracted the vile desire of disease of desire".

Truth is the highest quality on earth. All the ten Gurus stressed this point. Guru Nanak said, "He is a true dealer in horses who breeds the horses of Truth, stores wealth of virtue to meet the needs of the way; full of unfailing faith that, in the abode of the Formless, he shall share its bliss".

On various occasions the Guru talks of formlessness of the divinity. For instance, Guru Nanak says emphatically to his disciples, "He (God) cannot be installed like an idol, no man can shape His likeness'. He made himself, and maintains Himself, on His heights unstained forever".

Guru Nanak says again, "Conceit is the ruin of the soul, slander darkens the mind, power breeds tyranny. The tender hearted are pure, they who have knowledge are humble".

In the Sikh religion, as also in many other Indian religions the Gurus have a unique place. They are the highest, at par with God himself. Guru Ram Das says,

> The human body is a city, the rarest of gems and rubies there await thee,
> Acquire them by devotion and service to the Satguru.

God dwells in every heart. Similarly Guru Amar Das Says,

> In the body is everything,
> Higher real and nether world.
> In thy body resides the Almighty and Himself,
> who sustaineth all.
> In thy body are gems, rubies, and storehouses of devotion
> In this body is the treasure of *Nam* (the word of God)
> Which is obtained only by the grace of the Guru.

This is exactly the echo of what the Great Nanak observed earlier. He said, Guru, who is God, do thou worship with all jolly heart and soul; for giveth He life and faith, and sustaineth He all.

Because we all are born in this World only of divine will, Nanak Devji says,

> Birth and death are the laws of life,
> O, Brother, we come and go according to Divine Command.

A really dedicated devotee is always blissful. Guru Nanak says,

> The true saint of God knows Him nigh,
> all the hours of day and night.
> And sunset to him is the will of God,
> And all that the Lord ordains.

Guru Teg Bahadurji says, "From sin, He is redeemer, of the lost, He is the guide". Seventh Guru Arjan says, "The disciple who obeys at the Guru's feet, and patiently obeys the Guru's orders and abandons his will to the True Guru - such a man's doing shall prosper."

The Sikh religion is easy to follow. One has to utter the Holy Name with a pure mind. Nanak Devji says, "Priceless is His gifts - *Nam*. Priceless His marks upon them. Priceless His mercy and Priceless His will, How beyond price He cannot be expressed". From his personal experiments Guru Nanak has realised

> 'When the sound of His Name fills the heart,

All bliss and salvation is its reward;
Nanak says the truth - without His Priceless Name,
There is no release from bondage'.

To quote Guru Arjan, the great Saint poet,
I crave from Thee Lord, the gifts of Thy Name,
Nothing else will abide with me.
Kingdoms, gold, sensual delights
Vanish like the shadow cast by a tree,
The man who pursues shadows pursues vanities.

Very much in tune with the *Bhagavad Gita* Guru Arjan said "The soul is eternal and cannot be destoryed, it is neither born nor does it die".

With all humility and limited knowledge, I place before the readers in these few pages the secular thoughts of the Great Sikh Gurus:

1. Guru Nanak (1459 - 1539)
2. Guru Angad (1504 - 1552)
3. Guru Amar Das (1479 - 1577)
4. Guru Ram Das (1534 - 1581)
5. Guru Arjan (1563 - 1606)
6. Guru Har Gobind (1595 - 1644)
7. Guru Har Rai (1630 - 1661)
8. Guru Har Kishan (1656 - 1664)
9. Guru Teg Bahadur (1621 - 1675)
10. Guru Gobind Singh (1666 - 1708)

I firmly believe none of them is dead. They are very much with us with their great message of Love, Truth and Divinity.

I owe a great debt of gratitude to Justice Ranjit Singh Sarkaria, a learned scholar, deeply interested in spiritual and ethical thought, for having gone through the manuscript and making learned suggestions for imporvement.

I am also grateful to Shri S.J. Balasubramaniam for his valuable suggestions.

Respected Giani Zail Singhji has chosen to bless my humble effort. His thought - provoking Foreword is the outcome of his deeply religious mind, his great reverence for the Gurus, and his kind affection for the author. I am too overwhelmed by his kindness and love to express thanks in my inadequate language.

I must record my gratitude to Shri B.P. Garg and Shri Satyendra Nath Sarkar who have produced the book at a short notice.

Vivek Ranjan Bhattacharya

Contents

Foreword vii

Introduction xi

1. Sikhism
A Full-fledged Religion 1

2. Concept of Religion
As Realised by Guru Nanak 9

3. Secular Thoughts
Hallmark of the Sikh Gurus 25

4. Guru Nanak
Apostle of Secularism 29

5. Guru Angad Dev
Paragon of Selfless Service 57

6. Guru Amar Das
Man of Letters and Action 72

7. Guru Ram Das
Builder of the Holy City 89

8. Guru Arjun Dev
Compiler of Adi Granth 104

9. Guru Har Gobind
Lord of Spiritual and Secular Domains 120

10. Guru Har Rai
The Conformist 126

11. Guru Teg Bahadur
Hallowed Martyr 131

12. Guru Gobind Singh
Warrior Saint 139

Epilogue 151

1

Sikhism
A Full-fledged Religion

Religion is the manifestation of the divinity already in man. By religion we mean a particular system of faith and worship. It is through attuning the mind that a man can achieve unison with the infinite. True religion is the foundation of society, the basis on which all true civilisations had rested in the past, will rest in future and is resting today. Religion is equally the basis of private virtue and public faith of the happiness of the individual.

When a group of people lend their common emotional support and firm belief in any system of thought it becomes a religion. All religions throughout the world have had their beginning from the realised experiences of pathfinders. A number of followers had been following them, preserving them and sometime preaching them. That is the basic characteristic of religion.

Religion in its purity is not so much a pursuit as a temper; or rather it is a temper leading to the pursuit of all that is high and holy. "Its foundation is faith, its action, work; its temper, holiness; its aim obedience to God in improvement of self and benevolence to man". Religion cultures love. It has rightly been observed by a great philosopher that "take away God and religion, and men live to no purpose, without proposing any worthy and considerable end of life to themselves".

A saintly scholar has rightly defined the most significant characteristic of religion. He has rightly observed, "True religion shows its influence in every part of our conduct; it is like the sap of a living tree which penetrates the most distant boughs".

Sikhism is a religion. It has its own ritual which is followed strictly by the devotees of Guru Nanak. It has definitely cast responsibility even into outward observances like serving the poor, feeding the faithful in community kitchen, Langar, Sangat (religious congregation) and helping the poor. All Sikhs had been directed by Guru Nanak Devji to earn their living and avoid begging.

If one duly attended to one's religion and properly discharged one's religious duties I think the preaching of the word would not be the common instrument of conversion. In Sikh religion the word has the greatest significance. "Shabada is the most fundamental concept of Sikhism; it is related with the concept of God, Universe and Man. All other concepts of Sikhism can be rightly interpreted only by understanding what Shabada means." One must scientifically approach the matter. It is directly connected with the theories of Evolution and Creation. The ancient Scriptures also observed thousand of years ago Shabda Brahma, Shabada of the Sikhs is God personified.

The great Guru observed in his ecstatic state, "One word and the whole universe came into being. And rivers of life gushed forth." The religion of the Sikhs is based on this great foundation. Nanak Devji repeatedly said:

> "God is Word and Word is God.
> The word is thine O Lord
> And thou art of thyself,
> Why should then we dwell in doubt."

The energy of sound was the first manifestation of God. "God is thus, Holy Word, *shabada,* and light *jot.* This primordial sound is unstruck music, *anhad shabada,* that still sings in the space and is audible to those who can deeply concentrate".

Ancient sages described this as the eternal *anahata dhavani* regularly. He himself has recorded, "Unstruck music singeth in my mind as it is imbued with the love of the Lord".

God manifested Himself in this *anahata dhvani.* Therefore, Guru Nanak's religion, basically and scientifically is a religion where the first brick of the mighty edifice had been this *shabada* which is the essence of the universe". This is also the realisation of the ancient seers who went to the source and described, in all the *Upanisads* as *Om*. Guru Nanak Devji also joins this great lineage and observes:

"*Omkar* is He who created Brahma
Omkar is He who created consciousness
Omkar is He who created mountains
Omkar is He who created the *Yugas*, the light,
Hear yea, the meaning of the word *Om*
Which indeed is the essence of the Three Worlds".

This is exactly repetition of ancient concept of *Nad Brahma* or *Shabada Brahama*. This is the key to the religious discipline of the entire Sikh philosophy. So the word *Omkar* in the *Adi Granth* means "transcendent and immanent Lord". The author discussed this point with some modern saints including Ma Anandamayee. She unhesitatingly followed the version of Guru Nanak Devji and observed *Akshara Brahma* concept of the *Srimad Bhagavad Gita* is another description of the same idea of *Shabada Brahama* or *Nad* (Sound) *Brahma*.

Guru Nanak says :

"From the air began the life
And from God, the System,
The Word is the Guru
And the mind attuned to it was the disciple."

A great scholar Dr. Gill observes, "Since *Shabada* and God are synonymous, Guru Nanak was God Himself. So in Sikh scriptures, the word Guru is used for Godhead also".

Guru Nanak says :

There is but one Word uttered by the only Guru
So reflect on his Word alone
True is this storehouse of knowledge
True are its wares
The jewels found in it.
It is by the Guru's grace that we are blessed with the word
The true word is known the Four Ages,
Yea, the true one is himself true.

Finally Guru Nanak Dev gives the immortal religion of Sikhism the main substance of the faith.

He says :

"The Word is the Guru
the Guru is the Word,
In the Word are contained all the elixirs",

So *Shabada* is the all-important feature in the Sikh religion.

Guru Says :

"Through Words we meditate and praise God,
And procure knowledge and sing the virtues of God".

Dr. Gill observes, "*Shabada* has various meanings in Sikhism as God, *Nam,* Primordial sound, Holy Word, Scriptures and *Guru.* The concept has immense importance for a Sikh".

Guru Nanak says :

"The three worlds of God
Are within the sway of the Words,
Through the Words is carried on discourse in the *Vedas,*
The Words reveal what is written in The *Shastras,*
The *Smritis* and the *Puranas.*
Through the words the subtle music
And thoughts of *yogis* are appreciated
Through the words is told the way of deliverence
And thoughts of fear and doubt are blown,
Through the words the way of piety, religion
And good action is described
All that is seen is the Universe
Is under the sway of the words
But not the Transcendent Lord
Who is beyond their reach"

Later Gurus carried this idea further by their revised guidance where they have said "Fashion your mind anew according to the Word of the *Guru."*

The Sikh religion is basically a full-fledged, altogether different religion although there are many common features between Hinduism and the Sikh religion.

Guru Nanak rejected Hindu rituals. He himself observed:

"I have appeared in this world to indicate the way unto men.
I have rejected all sects and only know

One God whom I recognise in the earth,
The heavens and all directions.

Guru Nanak vehemently decried and denounced mere formal worship in the various sects and religions and outright condemned mere rituals and ceremonials as the gateway to heaven.

He told the Hindus:

"*Brahma* who came into the world repeating the *Vedas*
Cannot describe him
Shiva and countless gods and goddesses standing at
Thy gate praise Thee."
(Macanliffe: *Sikh Religion.* Vol I, p 128)

He told the Muslims.

"Merely reading the scriptures does not
Free the mind from anxiety.
If for a moment thou restrainest thy mind
God will appear before thee."
(Ibid. p 177)

Everything else, except the uttering of the Holy Name, is false. The Guru says,

'False are rings, false are subjects,
False the whole world,
False are mansions, false palaces,
False those who dwell in them
False is gold, false silver,
False he who weareth them,
False the body, false the raiment,
False peerless beauty,
False husbands, false wives, they pine away and become dust
(Ibid., p 130)

To him the Name and the Lord were one and he made no distinction between the two. The Sikhs deprecate all forms and formalities and give new definitions to words. He was asked clearly to define his religion.

Nanak Dev himself gave description of his new faith,

(My) Religion consisteth not in a patched coat
Or in the blowing of the horns,
Religion consisteth not in mere words

Religion consisteth not in visiting the tomb or places of cremation
of sitting in attitudes of contemplation,
Religion consisteth not in wandering in foreign countries,
Or in bathing in places of pilgrimage
Abide pure amid the impurities of the world,
Thus shall then find the way to religion.

To Guru Nanak, Name (the holy *Naam*) is the teacher and the Name is the only pathway. "There is no other road but the Name, and that is the only door in this *Kaliyug*".

This, incidentally, was also the motto and message of the entire *Bhakti Movement*that flooded whole of India creating a new perception of God-realisaiton. Mahaprabhu Chaitanya also preached the same Gospel. So, quite correctly, a saint scholar has observed, "Here was a gospel that had many points in common with what the earlier saints and those who followed him had said. And while praising the Name he emphasised on the gospel of devotion with which the Name is to be remembered. To him the Name and the Lord is the attitude of a true *Bhakta*. This is apparent in his lines which to some extent are nearer to Mira Bai in our own country and to the writings of St. Teresa and other mystics of the West. There is the same agony and the pang of separation."

The Name and the word are the main keynotes to spiritualist perception of Sikhism. Dr. Mcleod writes, "Guru Nanak's emphasis is wholly upon the concept of the word (*Sabad*) as the vehicle of revelation. Inevitably, the word is described by him more in terms of what it does than in terms of what it actually is. This is entirely natural as it is the function which concerns him and it is in experience that it is to be known rather than in any truly intellectual sense. The function of the *Word* is that it provides the means whereby man can know both God and the path which leads to Him, the means whereby the individual may secure release from his bonds and so attain unity with God. Again and again the word is declared to be the essential means of salvation. It is for Guru Nanak, the revelation of God and so the only proper object of man's contemplation. By contemplation of the Word and by the total conforming of one's life to its dictates the man is brought under control, self-centredness is cast out, the individual grows ever nearer to God until ultimately perfected in His likeness, he passess into a condition of union which transcends death and the cycle of transmigration" (Mcleod, W.H.: *Guru Nanak and the Sikh Religion*, p 192)

Guru Nanak, after his realisation, like a sage of the Upanisads, describes God as follows:

> He has neither form, nor material sign,
> But he is revealed through the true Word, *Sabad*
> By the Guru's leading he obtains salvation
> And is no longer bound (to the wheel of transmigration)
> Meditating on the Word *(Sabad)*
> *Repeating the Name of God he is released*
> *Without the Word (Sabad)* one is condemned to wander
> Worldly affections cause many to sink (in the ocean of Existence)
> O Man, apply your understanding to the Word *(Sabad)*
> And cross over.
> He who has not followed the Guru
> And so has not understood the divine Name
> (Such a person)
> Continues to transmigrate.
> Nanak, the Lord,the truecreater is known by means of the Word (Sabad)
> (Ibid, pp 192-93)

The word *Sabad*stands by itself as the personification of the Guru. It has been observed by a great scholar on Sikhism, "the latter may be regarded as the characteristic form, for the use of *Sabad by itself normally assumes its connection with the Guru. The form may be Guru ka Sabad,* the Gurus Word, or it may be *Guru Sabad*, the Guru Word. The latter carries us nearer the true meaning, for it brings out the basic identity of the two terms. The development of this point must, however, wait the section devoted to the Guru and in the meantime we must continue to use the expression the Guru's word or the Guru's *Sabad*".

This Guru's *Sabad* or *Guru Vani* is the quintessence of the Sikh religion. The Guru's word is the main guideline, like in any religion, also to the Sikhs.

Guru Nanak says,

> The word of the Guru is the inner music,
> The word of the Guru is the highest scripture

The word of the Guru is all-pervading
The Guru is *Shiva*
The Guru is *Vishnu*
The Guru is *Brahma*
The Guru is *Parvati*, the Mother Goddess.

Nanak Devji adds further,
Under the Guru's instructions
His knowledge is acquired,
Under the Guru's instruction
Man learns that God is everywhere".

(Selected from the Sacred Writing of the Sikhs)

The Guru has a tremendously high position in the spiritual life of a Truth Seeker.

Guru Nanak says,
Only that man finds peace of mind
Who meets the true Guru
And enshrines the name of God
and that too, Nanak in his heart
If God bestows His Grace.

(Asa di var)

He has neither form, colour, nor material sign,
But he is revealed through the true Word, *Sabad*.

2

Concept of Religion As Realised by Guru Nanak

Just as Bhagwan Mahavira systematised the entire Jaina philosophy culling ideas from the earlier great *Tirthankaras*, so also Guru Govind Singh, the Tenth Guru organised the ideas of the earlier nine Gurus and put the whole discipline under the banner of the Sikh religion. The first Guru, Guru Nanak Devji was a forerunner in the *Bhakti Movement* and was a pioneer who had struck a death knell to the time long caste system. Guru Nanak Devji can be described as a Prophet but not a Sikh because the meaning of the word is derived from Shisay which means a disciple. He is the first Guru and the entire faith is based mainly on the realised Truth as preached and practised by the great saint. He is the father of this great religion which has definitely given fresher outlooks to the concept of religion in India.

Guru Nanak Devji had not only introduced fresher ideas in the realm of religion but he was a pioneer in the field of great many social reforms. He did these things without any special effort. Although he had no intention of being a social reformer - his only aim in life was God-realisation - he had become one. His ideas were most practical and instead of preaching them he himself experimented them in practice.

Guru Nanak Devji was a born poet. Even though he had not preached any thing on his new faith yet he has gone down in history as one of the pioneers of Punjabi literature. Next only to Baba

Farid, who too was a born poet, Guru Nanak played the most vital role in flowering and enriching the Punjabi literature.

Both the saints, Baba Farid and Guru Nanak Devji, were enlightened souls and both would utter their realised Truth spontaneously in poetry!

This was a new thing for the masses. So long, religious discourses were restricted only to Sanskrit. Now, because it was in local language - Punjabi - even ordinary people could understand it. This is very much like Lord Buddha's spreading the message of peace and universal brotherhood of man in Pali.

Guru Nanak Devji would have composed poems on the spot with the most sublime thoughts of Indian philosophy. In fact, his ideas were so lofty and expressions so simple that it would touch any human mind without any difficulty. Some of the ideas of the great saint had greatly influenced the world poet Rabindranath Tagore to the extent that many of them sound as if they are mere translation of the poems of Nanak Devji.

In his childhood Tagore used to attend prayers in the Gurudwara at Dalhousie where he had accompanied his learned spiritually advanced father Maharisi Devendranath Tagore. The scriptures and especially the songs from *Guru Granth Sahibji* as sung or recited in the Gurudwaras had left a permanent imprint on the mind of child Rabindranath and echoed later on in many of his poems exclusively on the Sikh Gurus including Guru Banda and Guru Govind Singh.

There are long poems by Tagore which are mere translations of the original poems by Guru Nanak Devji. He also composed special poems in the praise of the founder of the Sikh religion.

Right from his childhood Guru Nanak Devji had a deep yearning for exploring the Truth. His mystic mind would be most unaffected by the surroundings and he would be least interested in the worldly things. Surprisingly, he would never face any adverse situation. Some invisible power would see to his full protection from any danger.

Once his father sent him with some money to get some salt at wholesale rate from a dealer. The idea was to settle the child in business. This was an effort to gain some experience for the young lad.

On the way the young man met some mendicants, who after long pilgrimage, were all hungry. So the young man made the best use of the money by feeding the mendicants. He was more than rewarded by the ecstasy in the whole body and mind.

He would be busy in deep meditation when asked by the parents to look after the herds of bufaloes who would destroy the greenfield of grain of neighbours who happened to be wealthy land -lord. When the landlord with all his fury and fume sends for the young lad, he pleads not guilty and requests the feudal lord to visit his field. Lo behold, nothing has happened ! The field is as normal as ever before !

Lad Nanak would muse in lonely corner and would not be interested in the sports or games by children of his age. His parents, who were quite attached to the child, on noticing this got terribly worried about the child's future. They wanted the child to become a rich man doing business.

Guru Nanak Devji did not believe in idolatory. He did not believe in any sort of caste system. He did not think that religion was the monopoly of any particular section of members of society. He did not find any difference between Hinduism and Islam. To him there was only one God. To be precise, the whole philosophy, silently was a challenge to the existing Brahminical system of religion. He did not believe in any rituals. It was very much like Lord Buddha's challenge to the monopoly of the Brahminism.

So a learned scholar has aptly observed, "Although the fathers of Brahminism have long been firmly riveted on India, attempts to loosen them date back to Buddhism and were renewed by many religious and social reformers from whom Sikhism borrowed ideas and even devotional hymns. Such were Jaidev, composer of *Geet Govind* (translated by Edwin Arnold) who *circa* A.D. 1100 taught that Yoga was worthless in comparison with God's worship in thought, word and deed; Ramanand, at the close of the 14th Century, freed his followers, from caste restrictions; a little later Kabir (1398) denounced idolatory and ritualism. Nearly a century later in 1469, was born Nanaka the first founder of Sikhism, contemporary with Luther. His name means "he who was born at the home of his mother's parents" and it lay at Talwandi, near Lahore of a Khatri family, Sikh account of his descent makes him a reincarnation of King *Videha Janaka,* the great patron of Kshatriya Upanisads. The tradition may contain a grain of Truth". Guru Nanak, like his contemporary Chaitanya had his faith in monotheism. He taught "the worthlessness of religious vestments, of ostentations, prayer and penance, pilgrimage and fames."

It was a great departure from the age old path. Guru Nanak proclaimed loudly that "all men had a right to search for knowledge of God, irrespective of caste. He was quietest and though we have no authentic biography of him, we may conjecture that his life and doctrines did not expose him to persecution, and we hear nothing of any efforts to suppress his teachings. He was employed by a Muslim and was married leaving on his death in 1533 two sons, Sri Chand and Lakshmi Das, both Hindu names. Nanak, however, had designated as his successor in his spiritual message the Guruship, another Kshatri, Lehna, who took the name Angad. To Guru Angad Granth Sahib in which he embodied what he had learnt from Guru Nanak, adding devotional reflections of his own. To mark the sacred character of the work, he is said to have invented Gurumukhi, the Guru's tongue the holy script of the Sikhs by modification of the Sharada alphabet. Dying in 1552 Angad too, like Guru Nanak, excluded his sons and designated the Kshatri Amar Das as his successor.

The Sikh religion is a part of the mainstream of culture that represents Indian philosophy. Nanak's approach to God-realisation was an ideal secular one. He did not restrict his religiosity to any particular sect. He had a wider vision. That was universalising the concept of God-realisation. The approach too was different. He stressed on service to man. He stressed on community lunch. This Langar or concept of community lunch is one of the greatest gifts of the Sikhs in the socio-religious life in India. It, not only helps the poor to have some morsel of Food for the day (the system is still popular throughout India and is spreading steadily among other religious groups also) it levels people of different status. The status consciousness or egotism of the so - called elite or the rich is removed by this unique system. Historians of eminence like Dr. R.C. Majumdar consider this as the greatest contribution of Nanak, followed up by his disciples and the order in the social reform that has done away with the decadent caste system. In this community lunch people from all sects, creeds and regions are most welcome. This is one of the most practical approach to secularism in action. Gradually the ideas of Nanak are spreading through translation in action silently and is showing many path-finders the proper way to God-realisation through service.

One of the greatest messages of the Guru is that "one must earn one's own bread" everyday. It had found expressions in great modern philosophers like Thoreau and Tolstoy. This is the path through which a nation can be self-reliant. Hard work has been the motto of all the Sikh Gurus. That is the main secret of success in all spheres of life of the Sikhs spread all over the world. Secularism cannot just appear from the sky. The way the great Sikh Guru started the socio-economic reforms were leading to secularism automatically. Idolatory, caste system, the rituals, the restrictions to Sanskrit mantras, all these were hurdles to the ordinary men to God-realisation. They were eager to taste the nectar of divine message. But unfortunately the door was closed to them by the prevalent system. No body was to be blamed, of course. It was existing for ages and nobody ever challenged it but for the enlightened Buddha more than two thousand five hundred years ago. The system was finding its own way especially by a team of priests whose livelihood depended on the exploitation of the innocent and ignorant masses. The entire Bhakti Movement was an eye opener. In this background Nanak's appearance as a Prophet was a most welcome event. He came as a great *Messhiah* of peace and universality of mankind. This immediately caught the imagination of the people who always hanker for a novelty in approach, especially if it has anything to do with spirituality. He was against any sect but his words, his speeches, messages, all had been deeply drenched with spiritualism. No wonder in no time Sikhism had spread as a new faith in the entire national arena. With its secular approach it steadily spread far and near. To quote an eminent scholar, "The growth of the Sikh faith is a living embodiment of the secular traditions of our great country. The various streams that merge in the Statements of this faith transcend caste and class boundaries to symbolise a universal human vision. The Sri Adi Grantha carries streams of contributions by the Sufi Saints and others, wandering socio-religious reformers."

A very important aspect of the teaching of Guru Nanak is his tremendous respect for each individual. Dignity to man, humility and deep reverence for the individual are the main aspects of the thought process of this great prophet of India. He shuns minor divisions or compartmentalisation in the name of Hindus or Muslims - and at that time these two were the major religions of India. He believes only in Truth, that is God, the great Guru says,

> There is one God
> He is the Supreme Truth,
> He the Creator
> Is without fear and without hate.
> He, the omnipresent
> Pervades the Universe.

(*Japji* translated by Khushwant Singh)

It sounds very much like the echo of the Upanisads.

In *Japji* we get the substance of the sublime thoughts of the Prophet. There are many translations. One of the authentic versions is that by Sardar Khushwant Singh, who has written also the History of the Sikhs in two volumes.

When one reads the Japji one feels he is reading the ancient Upanisad. For instance at one place Guru Nanak says:

> He is not born,
> Nor does he die to be born again.
> By His grace shalt thou worship Him
> Before time itself.
> There was Truth
> When time began to run its course.
> He was the Truth.
> Even now, He is the Truth
> And ever more shall Truth prevail.

(*Japji*)

Guru Nanak had attained extraordinary intuitive power. He had proved that on many occasions. Once when confronted with

Muslim priests who asked him whether he was a Hindu or a Muslim, the saint in his state of ecstasy said "What? There is nothing as Hindus nor there is anything as Muslims. We are all children of God."

Once he joined them in their prayer but suddenly questioned the chief priest why he was thinking of buying and selling of horses in Kabul. All were stunned. The chief priest was convinced that the wandering monk was not any ordinary man. It was here that the saint described how to become a real Muslim. He said, "If compassion be thy mosque, faith thy prayer- mat and honest living thy Quran, and modesty thy circumcision., contentment thy fast, then verily thou art a true Muslim. Let good deeds be thy Kaaba, and Truth thy Prophet and thy prayer be for God's Grace. And thy rosary be of His will then, sayeth Nanak, God will keep the honour."

Even five hundred years ago the Prophet had the most scientific approach of reason and rationale. When he clearly indicated that he did not believe either in Hinduism nor in Islam, he was obviously asked then what was his faith ? The reply was simple, straight and most modern. The prophet said," I am a mere man made of five elements.'

The most outstanding feature of Sikhism is its emphasis on not renouncing worldly activities. "A Sikh believes implicitly in the teachings of the ten Gurus and the Guru Granth Sahib. Of the ten Gurus, three in particular - Nanak, Arjan and Gobind Singh - have left a deep impression of their personalities on Sikhism. Guru Nanak (1469-1539), founder of the Sikh religion, preached the unity of Godhead, the obligation of leading a pure life, the abolition of caste and the futility of ritual and form. There was nothing new or startling about this, the common theme of all the reformers of the time. Nanak's real greatness lay in the fact that, in an age troubled by doubts and uncertanties his words rang out loud and clear like a trumpet. His fundamental teachings are contained in his verses known as *Japji*, rightly considered to be the epitome and indeed the main inspiration of the Guru Granth Sahib".

Scholars have compared it with Buddhism and Jainism which developed out of Hinduism and a challenge to the Brahaminical monopoly. Religion which was restricted only to the priest class so long got released from this limited sphere and opened its doors to all who were interested in spirituality. Its main emphasis on castelessness is its greatest contribution to the cultural history of India. However, the same scholars also opine that "the lines which distinguish Sikhism from Hinduism are not sharp and clear cut, the basic ethical values in the two being more or less the same."

Japji is one of the most sacred scriptures of India. It is "the ontology, the epistemology, the ethics and the whole theology." To know the inner secret and the message of the great faith preached and practised by Guru Nanak Devji one must study this all important holy book without fail. Dozens of books giving sermons and details of the faith will fail to satisfy a seeker of Truth what the Japji offers in capsule form. It is like the sutras of the Vedas. It has been aptly observed that translation of Japji are in galore, but there are only a few extent, reflect the personality of the translator and the work of a prophet like Japji is bound to lose much of its beauty and intensity in a translation by a mortal being." It is very ture. Why only a translation ? Even the original version of the Japji will not be really realised so easily by an ordinary reader who does not have a deep religious perception and whose mind is not fitted enough emotionally and philosophically ready and qualified properly to receive the great message. The mind cannot receive the highest sublime thought. One must be fitted enough emotionally and philosophically ready and qualified properly to receive the great message. The mind cannot receive it till it is fully prepared and cultured for it.

It has been said that "Japji is in Pauris which literally means steps. In all there are 38 Pauris, with Sloka in the beginning and a Sloka at the end. Guru Nanak Sahib has devoted the first seven Pauris to Self consecration. They describe four cultures which purify the emotions of the mind."

Guru Nanak stresses the ethical aspect of a man's spirituality. He guides mankind to keep the medium of reception of the spiritual power, that is the mind must always be absolutely clean and clear. It must be a clean medium so that message transmitted can easily be received. For this, after this enlightenment, like the Buddha, Nanak suggests the following steps :

1. Discrimination
2. Dispassion
3. Deep Devotion
4. Development of inner light or consciousness
5. The three Highways - Trimarga

In addition, the prophet, like a true Vedantist recommends the inner manifestation of the six jewels. These are Sama, Dama, Shraddha, Samadhan, Uparamata and Titiksha. The prophet clearly observes, "O man, there lie buried within your psyche jewels. You must purify your Tamasic emotions by taking the help of a competent Guru, otherwise, hostile forces will creep imperceptibly through the breaches made thereby."

Liberation is the seventh step. The mind must be liberated from other thoughts to receive the divine light. It must be pure, clear, clean and without any fear or egotism.

This is followed by further nineteen steps or Pauris. These nineteen steps may be categorised under four disciplines which are :-

1. Shravana (by listening)
   (eighth to eleventh steps)
2. Manana (by meditation)
   (twelfth to fifteenth steps)
3. Nidhyasana (by absorption or assimilation)
   (Sixteenth to Nineteenth)
4. The substance of the aphorisms of Sama Veda especially Chhandogya Upanisad leading to the great conclusion Thou art that Tat tvam asi (Twentieth to Twenty Sixth Steps)

It is surprising that great saints, be they ancient, medieval or modern, after their enlightenment, come to the same conclusion and confirm the description of Truth, the Infinite and the Brahma exactly the same way. Their knowledge was never bookish. They never even cared to go through these scriptures. One is stunned for instance, to listen to Nanak uttering the same truth as described in the Chhandogya Upanisad which perhaps he never cared to study. In our modern days we also find many great divine souls, foremost among them being Sri Ramakrishna Paramahansa, who was, so to say, almost an unlettered God-man but whatever he uttered out of his inner-enlightenment was exactly similar to the thoughts as expressed in the Vedas, Upanisads and Srimad Bhagavad Gita. This is the finer chord which has been responsible for the continuity of Indian culture, the most ancient and yet so modern. It is the immortal soul of Indian spirituality which has emitted itself out of long deep meditation of great prophets like Nanak, Chaitanya, Sri Ramakrishna and more than a few hundred of divine personalities. Many of them were highly learned even from the point of view of scholarliness of worldly knowledge but that bookish knowledge is like imitation glittering gold which only sparkle but is hardly of any intrinsic value of everlasting philosophical guideline to the realm of spirituality, especially leading to God-realisation.

After the 26 Pauris or steps the human mind reaches the sublime state of divine bliss. The Guru himself describes the state of "the highest pitch of sublimity." The Guru himself writes,

"The one remains, the many change and pass,
Heaven's light for ever shines Earth's
Life, like a dome of many coloured glass
Stains the white radiance of Eternity."

The next five Pauris (twenty eighth to thirty first) describe the terrestrial life of the evolved being who has now become one with the One.

But this is not all. Even after one attains this highest state of divinity one has to continue. There is continuous need for further Japam and surrender - one must get God's grace, without which nothing is possible. This is described in the thirty second and thirty third Pauris. Japam and surrender are the two common features of God-realisation in any major religious discipline. Grace of God, popularly known as Kripa is a must. One must be completely humble. One must shun one's all egotism and only pray to the Almighty with all humility. In fact this state comes automatically to a saint as it did also with the great contemporary of Nanak Dev, Mahaprabhu Sri Chaitanya. Japam and surrender, all alone can lead a Truth seeker to attain God-realisation. The other rituals are merely auxiliary adjuncts.

So the scholar, who analysed the Japji rightly observed, "How beautifully Guru Sahib shows that the psychic change demands devestiture of the mask of ignorance. Notwithstanding purification, the egoistic, mental and physical movements prolong the old inferior consciousness and there is constant need for a spirit of adoration of the personal aspect of spirit whenever the Jivanmukta, the liberated soul is not absorbed in communion with Absolute.

The soul's relative existence is described in the thirty fourth to thirty seventh Pauris. Guru Sahib also describes the stages life after death - the "celestial life" in the three last Pauris. In the final Pauri Guru Sahib has "epitomised Japji", so that is most important as that gives the substance of his entire philosophy as felt by him. Guru Nanak's greatest message to the world in the realm of spirituality forms an important event in the experiments of God-realisation history not only in India but it is a part of history of world culture and should be spread far and wide. He was an enlightened Godman with a wide vision of life and not restricted to any particular sect, caste, society or group. He belongs to the whole of humanity. He definitely does not belong to the Sikh community only. He belongs to the whole world.

The Guru says, "The triple mode viz. Sattva (light and good), Rajas (passion and desire) and Tamas (darkness and ignorance) rules out nature. We have to become witnesses of its working within us - adjoining first of all the last two components viz. rajas and tamas, and developing the first one, viz, sattva. Uptil now the change has to be brought by the will of the mental being within us through personal effort. Later on this Sattva is also to be converted into the triple divine equivalent of Sat (supreme repose and calm), Chit (illumination and knowledge) and Ananda (bliss and ecstasy). This comes with the mental being having been replaced by the deeper psychic soul through divine grace".

Who will say that this is not from the Upanisad ? Enlightened knowledge reveals in the same manifestation. So one sounds as the echo of the other. Truth is universal and the same. Scholars will guide a truth seeker to the thirteenth step (Pauri) of the Guru Sahib's immortal Japji. He does it as"an illumined mind". Japji has to be recited at dawn and only after a bath.

In the Japji the great Guru says, after a mind is illumined, "action proceed not from the instincts of flesh and emotions but from the spiritualised self and divine Supramental Truth, Consciousness and Bliss force within us. Here dawns on the horizon an apocalyptic vision which Guru Sahib so beautifully describes in twenty seventh Pauri. After face to face revelation of God, the evolved being who now has become operates as a conscious instrument of the Supreme Lord worker and follows His mandate, not doing work for satisfying his emotional desires but revelling in the obedience of the omnipotent will which Guru Sahib avers in thirty third Pauri. In other words he comes out to be the True coin which Guru Sahib described in the last Pauri of Japji. He shares the omniscient knowledge, enjoys the fathomless love and is submerged in the limitless ocean of the supreme Bliss of Existence".

Like all sages and seers of the Upanisads, the Guru assigns the highest importance to the mono-syllable OM. In Japji the Guru Sahib says just in the beginning "OM is the Vedic name of Nirgun Brahman - the immanent and transcendent aspect of God. Because OM represents three Gods AUM signifying Brahma (A), (U) Vishnu (M) Shiva. As distinguished from the three gods, the Guru Sahib puts one before OM signifying that God is one and singular. This the Guru did intentionally, because in his wisdom he wanted to avoid any sort of quarrel among the followers of different schools of Hindu faith.

God is one. "His name represents Truth - the cosmic Existence which exists in all forms, inorganic and organic, the plant and the animal creation".

Like all enlightened sages of India, Nanak Devji also stresses importance of renunciation (tyag). One must avoid desire to get divine light. This is the common teaching of all the immortal saints of the land. Guru Nanak says, "Hunger of worldly lust is not appeased, even if one were to secure, treasure load of worlds". In the same breath the Guru emphatically maintains, "Let a man possess one thousand or even a hundred thousand kinds of worldly wisdom, but not one will be of any avail in the other world".

One must surrender oneself to the supreme will of God. One must surrender oneself to the obedience of divine Law which is written large in our destiny in the form of Sanskaras and Praravda.

On renunciation Shri Guru says, "Renunciation of desires by surrender to the divine will is the central secret. Renunciation of personal desire leads to equality, accomplishing identity with the whole creation and delivering us from the dividing ego, bringing oneness. Thus trained, desire, that great unquiet harasser and troubler of the mind, that mighty forest fire, is extinguished and transformed into the pure ecstasy of the souls seeking beyond all craving and grief.

In the same Sloka (Pauri II) Guruji says, "So long as we desire we are the ego, enslaved to wants and bound to the dualities of grief and joy, pain and pleasure, success and failure, virtue and vice, good and evil. Our so - called free will is at bottom illusory, because it is the modes incorporated in our nature which express themselves as our personal will. The only free will in the world is the one divine will of which our nature is only the apparatus, for she is the master and creator of all other wills".

The divine will or manifestation is "indescribable". It is only through "divine will" that the Truth Seeker gets sublimity in the form of changes of the inner consciousness and nature". Only then a man becomes a Saint. Sri Aurobindo describes this state as Supramental State of Mind.

Only when a man gets enlightened he becomes truly humble, as we find in the case of all great saints like Chaitanya. Once Guru Nanak's son (who was not nominated as the spiritual heir by Nanak Dev) asked Guru Angad (the second Guru) why he was having long beard which almost crossed his waist. Angad immediately told the Guru's son (although he was senior in protocol) "Sir, this long beard is to clear the dust of your holy feet".

Such was the humility of a really enlightened saint. Angad got his training from Nanak Devji directly and had put Japji into practice in all spheres of his life. Like many ancient saints (Buddha and Mahavira Nanak Devji too believed in rebirth. Persons who are lucky get divine mercy and "others are made to wander forever in the circle of birth and death".

When a man is deeply engrossed in search of Truth and God-realisation, the Guru says from personal experience, "he would not talk in terms of I and mine".

Pavhari Baba whom Swami Vivekananda considered one of the greatest saints of India and whom he was almost accepting as his second Guru always spoke in third person. Self attainment is silent and secret. It is gradual and steady. One cannot expect it suddenly miraculously. "Self attainment is the secret, self knowledge is its means and increasing consciousness is the process. Effective knowledge must be achieved by a disciple from a Guru whose greatness is eulogised because he guides the disciple according to the proclivities predominant in the disciples nature, along one of the three paths of work, devotion or knowledge".

Ego is a great enemy of God - realisation. One has to shun this hurdle at any cost. Nanak Says, "One way of attaining this state when he will not talk in terms of I and mine is through deep devotion where the devotee pours himself into the Guru who for him is divinity."

This great place of the Guru is a common feature between the ancient scriptures and the philosophy of Nanak. The scriptures of ancient India describes the Guru as God personified - Gurur Brahma, Gurur Vishnu, Gururdevo Maheshwara, Gururdeva Param Brahama Tasmai, Sri Gurabay namo is the description of the spiritual pathfinder for thousands of years. Many saints confirm this conception.

A man who has ever tasted the nectar of God-realisation will never talk about himself. He will only chant the Holy Name of God. Nanak says, "When roots of insight go deep he cannot talk about anything else but the paradise of the Lord. His greatness and enchanting virtues. When a devotee is in trouble he remembers Him, he sees Him at once coming to solve the devotees difficulties.

In the Srimad Bhagwad Gita also Lord Krishna assures that he takes charge of all his disciples, who completely surrender themselves to Him. At the same time he also declares that he is always shadowing a disciple who takes His shelter. Ahang Bhakto Paradhino—I am a captive of a devotee. I am under bondage (dependent) on the devotee." Having developed celestial sight he envisages how the Lord creates bodies and then destroys them and chants praise of the Lord."

A real devotee feels the presence of God all the time. "He perceives His presence as operating from afar and chants His praise."

Guru Nanak,from self experience observes to the world of Truth seekers, "He sees his living, presence in closest proximity, and in joy sings His praise."

In the scriptures sages and seers of ancient times have clearly observed that He is beyond description. Nanak Devji also confirms, after his own enlightenment "It is beyond description. However, much one may describe it there will be no end of it." Shri Guru says "God is Truth. His songs of praise and love brings increasing consciousness of the Divine." God is beyond description, "Billions upon billions speak again and again over and over again (but cannot describe Him)".

The only thing that a truth-seeker may ask God to grant as a boon is of His constant presence. "As big the boon so big should be the offering, and this offering is that which entitles you to see His Court i.e. share the joy of His company."

The uttering of the Holy Name is an important feature of Sikh religion. This was the common message of the saints and pioneer of the Bhakti Movement. This made the God realisation easier for the common man who was quite ignorant about the details of the rituals as practised so long by the communities headed by the professional priests who were reigning supreme over the religious realm.

In the Japji the question is raised "What words are to be uttered from the mouth ?"

Guru Nanak's reply is "Such that hearing them He may bestow His love, in other words, such that the beloved Himself becomes the lover".

"And what is that offering and which are those words ?" Guru Nanak replies, "At the ambrosial hour chant the Name of the Lord and His glory."

Finally, he says, "He alone is true who is all, and all are in Him".

This is exactly the idea as reflected throughout the Srimad Bhagwad Gita. The only way to reach Him is through selfless service. This too is a common sermon by the great sages and seers of India. This is the highest teaching of their Vedanta.

Guru Nanak says that the second way to God realisation is through deep devotion. This devotion should be limitless and boundless. It should be single minded - devotion. This can be cultivated by constantly chanting the Holy Name of the Lord, "Who is repositary of all virtues".

The third way is divine wisdom. Nanak says, this can be attained by becoming Gurumukh by which he becomes one with the new syllable OM when he is personified with the Vedas and gets completely identified with God.

The power of the pathfinder, the spiritual preceptor or the guru is indescribable."Even if I knew, I could not put it in words. It is simply ineffable". "But one truth the Guru has brought home to me and that is the prayer "Grant me O Lord, who alone art the Master of all creation, that Thee I may never forget".

Bathing in a sacred pond is useless unless one can bathe in the "deep in the waves of His bliss". If I taste not the nectar of bathing in the bliss of His Name that bath for weary souls what use is by bathing."

One can get the right path only by listening to the Guru. Shri Guru Nanak Devji says, "One lesson Guru has taught me and that is the prayer,"Grant me, O Lord/thou who alone art the giver for the whole universe that I can chant unceasingly Thy Name."

3

Secular Thoughts Hallmark of the Sikh Gurus

Guru Nanak was secular to the core. In all his preachings he shunned class, caste and creed, and vehemently stressed on equality of humankind. He gave the highest respect to the divinity of man. He preferred sharing food with an honest carpenter than enjoying the best dishes offered by a feudal lord. To him purity of mind and soul had the best appreciation. The Guru had never distinguished between a Hindu and Muslim. In fact, his constant company was a Muslim, Mardana, who used to play on the rabab wherever the great saint-poet would sing his self-composed songs.

He went to the pilgrimage of both the Hindus and the Muslims and was confronted with many in Mecca and Madina where before the learned gathering he clearly expressed his firm faith in secular thoughts,the highest in realm of God-realisation.

The Guru did not have any faith in idolatory. He, however, never decried anybody's faith. He was much against superstition and blind faith. It is indeed quite interesting to note how the Saint single-handedly opposed the time honoured customs.

Once, while in Mecca, Nanak Dev was too tired. In his sleep the saint turned his feet toward the shrine of Kaaba. It was a place where the faithful ones sat in rapt attention in meditation. An Arab priest noticed it and protested: Who are you? You are a sinner. You have turned your feet towards God!

Nanak Dev did not lose his calm. He assured the priest, "Turn, O faithful one, these feet in the direction in which He is not". A great scholar, who too later on joined the monkhood, records, "Tradition assign a miracle on the occasion. As the priest in a rage dragged his feet in the opposite direction, the shrine followed the revolutions of the body."

A similar incidence had earlier taken place in Hardwar. When the pilgrims at Hardwar were offering prayer to Ganga Mayi, their face being turned towards the East, he approached them and inquired as to what they were doing. They replied that they were offering Tarpan to their forefathers who were dead and were in the other world. So he took up the advice and turning his face towards the West began to offer his prayers. The priests (the Pandas) were angry. They protested. They considered this as an unholy act. He replied , "My fields are situated in the Punjab in that direction, and it is hot season, my fields must be parched. I am trying to water them."

The Pandas were enraged. They said, "fool, how can the fields so far off be watered by sprinkling water here? At once he retorted, greater fools are you who think that by offering water oblations here the dead ancestors in the other world can be satisfied? He was not only upright, very confident about his action but was tremendously bold.

The Saint's outlook was so wide and imagination so broad that he did not allow them to be limited to these petty superstitions and time honoured rituals of blind faith without any basic reasoning. Similarly at Puri, once while the whole congregation was busy in offering Arati, prayer with earthen lamps with oil, a priest noticed Nanak, relaxing and resting. So out of curiosity he asked the wandering mendicant the reason for his absence from the mass prayers.

Prayer? With these small earthen lamps? He is worshipped by the sun, the moon and the stars. What shall I do with these earthern lamps?

Tagore translated the whole poem and got it published as his own in the collection of poems. It is used as a prayer song and has become a very famous Rabindra Sangeet. Tagore should have acknowledged it to Guru Nanak. It is in a classical style, and when sung in chorus as it is done normally it creates a divine atmosphere drenched with deep spirituality.

The point is, the Saint did not tread the old path. He invented his own. His ideas were new and original. Today they are all fully honoured and practised. So he was four hundred years in advance of his age. Guru Nanak did not spare the Brahmin priests for bigoted ideas. He did not spare the Moulvis, for their old, outdated rituals.

Guru Nanak Dev did love both the Hindus and the Muslims equally, although he did not favour their bigoted blind practices. Among the Hindus the great Saint hated, and was one of the pioneers to strike a death knell to, the caste system. He wanted all people to join the orchestra reciting the Holy Name of God. For the first time the door of God-realization was open to one and all. The old orthodox school never allowed the weaker members of society to enter the temples. He opposed the idea tooth and nail. The community kitchen, known popularly as the Langar is a symbol of the great Saint's thoughts of secularism.

He loved the Muslims too. Guru Nanak Dev once defined a Muslim as one "who hath effaced his ego completely". This was the creed of Nanak. To him there was no Muslim, no Hindus. In a sense he breathed pantheism of the Sufi minus his austerities and life of celibate anchorite. (Bankey Behari: Sufis, Mystics and Yogis in India, p214)

Guru Nanak's message of secularism was carried further by his successors. The second Guru, Guru Angad, was the saint who put it into practice by popularising the Langar, the community kitchen. "Langar played an important part in bringing unity among the masses. Everyone was equal in the Guru's kitchen and the princes and the nobles all sat together and ate the same food. The number of followers increased". They were from all sections of the community.

Guru Amar Das gave even more importance to the institution of Langar. He would say, "pahle pangat, picche sangat, "first sit in the kitchen, then seek the company of the Guru".

Guru Amar Das had an entirely secular approach. He wanted to enlighten specially the weaker section of the society.

Similarly Guru Ram Das, a poet of eminence, was secular to the core:

"All other sects are for worldly power
For wordly gains the foods and struggle
Subject to birth and death they stake life
I am the Lord's faction.
Who can look after me in this world and the next".

Arjun Dev was the greatest poet among the Gurus. His poems are drenched with the spirit of renunciation and secularism:

Uneasy feels the king who rules the world.
Even he will get relief if he loves the Name.
A man may possess million his desire will still be unbounded.
He would release from this desire by obtaining the wealth of Name:
The various enjoyments of the world will not allay his thirst
It could be appeased by drinking the nectar of the Name.
In the valley of death which man has to traverse alone
The Name will be with him to confront him".

Guru Hargovind was a secular saint who was a personal friend of the Moghul crown Prince Salim. He continued his friendship with Emperor Jahangir with whom he used to go on hunting expeditions. He too was well-known as a great secular pathfinder in the realm of spirituality. He was affectionately described by his disciples and admirers as Sacheha Padshah, the true king. During his popular religious authority he was so popular with both the Hindu and Muslim masses that there was a secret report about him to the Moghal Durbar about his "building a kingdom". Guru Arjan Das was already murdered. Now was the turn of Hargovind. The emperor turned hostile to him. All sorts of harassments made his life miserable. It was in the Mughal jail that his simplicity and pious life and learning attracted Jahangir's notice who not only let him set free but befriended him.

Guru Gobind Singh, the highly qualified tenth Guru, was the most secular among the Gurus. Details about his secular beautiful poems will be discussed in the chapter on the most important of the Sikh Gurus.

4

Guru Nanak
Apostle of Secularism

Guru Nanak is the founder of Sikhism. He was a great pathfinder in the spiritual realm of India. He banished caste system and struck the death knell to the orthodox school practising rituals. He was a pioneer of the Bhakti movement. He practised and preached equality of man before God. To him, "God is all pervading - "One Great and True Being." He was a great prophet with a vision of finding God in man.

Guru Nanak was born in April 1469* at Talwandi, a village in Punjab. He was a Khatri by caste. Nanak had shown the signs of spiritual inclination right from his childhood. He was a gifted poet, a talented student with a mind deeply absorbed in mysticism. His father Kalu was an accountant by profession. He was having a farm also.His mother was Tripta. Both were deeply religious, particularly the mother who looked to the child as a divine one.

Father Kalu showed concern about Nanak's moody outlook and tried to dissuade his son from spiritual leanings. He sent him to

---

* Born in the morning of the 3rd day of the light half of the month of Baisakh (Mid of April to Mid May) in year 1469 AD. Since olden times, it is celebrated on the day of the full moon in the month of Kartik (Oct.-Nov.)

the farm to look after the fields and to attend to other chores. Everybody could discern the absent-mindedness of the child.

The father did not hesitate even to admonish him. The more the pressure to live a materialistic life was imposed on Nanak, the more he was inclined towards his spiritual pursuit and exploring truth. Like Sri Ramakrishna, Guru Nanak also used to gather friends and use to sing chorus songs in praise of God. They were self-composed songs. He did not believe in any other power -physical, financial, or even medical - than God. He did not believe even in the power of medical practitioners who were sometimes called to cure his occasional illness. To the doctor he would say,

"The physician is sent for to prescribe a remedy; he taketh my hand and feeleth my pulse. The ignorant physician knoweth not that it is in my mind that the pain is."

He was deeply absorbed in divine thinking and did not believe that a human being could cure another human being. He did not accept any physical pain of the body and would publicly tell everybody that he had a pain no doubt. More than that it was rather the agony of the mind. That could not be cured by a doctor. It was something beyond the latter's capacity. It was his mental agony of separation from the Almighty. He would say, "My body is weeping and my soul is crying for Almighty. Can anyone of you cure that ? If you have any remedy for that you come and help me." He would always try to meditate only on God and he would say, "I feel first the pain of separation from God, then pang of hunger for contemplation of Him."

I also feel the pain which Death's powerful myrmidons may inflict. I feel pain that my body shall perish by disease:

> "O ignorant physician : Give me no medicine.
> Such medicine as thou hast, my friend, removeth not the pain I feel or the continued suffering of my body.
> I forgot God and devoted myself to pleasure; then this bodily illness befell me : the wicked heart is punished.
> O ignorant physician : Give me no medicine.
> As sandal is useful when it exhaleth perfume, a man is useful as long as he hath breath in his body. When the breath departeth, the body crumbleth away and becometh useless:

"No one taketh medicine after that. When man possesseth even a portion of the Name of the Bright one, his body shalt become like gold and his soul be made pure."

Child Nanak would prefer spending more time in his mystic mood in search of God than concentrating on the school text books. He learnt Hindi and composed poems in Hindi. He studied Persian too. A feudal lord of the village Raibular promised the child a high post if he would become specialised in Persian. In his compositions, Nanak frequently used Persian words. He had access to the masterly works of the Sufi mystic poets. In his childhood, Nanak was much fond of mixing with wandering monks and fakirs.

Nanak's father got him married at an early age to tie him down with family life. His wife Sulakhni had all the good qualities. He had two sons. He would frequently leave the house and go to the forest and concentrate peacefully. He was fond of solitude. Whenever he was in company of many, Nanak would divert their entire attention to group singing in praise of God.

The father lost all hopes of his son getting settled as a householder. Whenever the father would give him some money for trade purposes,the son would spend it on feeding the poor. The feudal lord of the village of Talwandi was an admirer of the Guru. He wanted to save the promising yogi from the clutches of his father. He was sent to Sultanpur with an offer of job.

Nanak's father-in-law was a senior official of the rank of a collector of revenue under the Governor. He wanted to get him settled at Sultanpur. Both the feudal Lord and the father-in-law Jai Ram, sent the young man to an official of the Governor, Daulat Khan. He was appointed as a Store Keeper. During those days, salary was paid in kind and Nanak was getting quite a substantial quantity. He was keeping for himself only a portion, and would distribute the rest to the Sadhus around. He was extremely popular among the poor and the needy. Mardana joined him as a "private servant, friend and companion in devotion." He used to accompany Nanak on the rebeck when the latter sang. A few more friends also followed him. "When their work for the day was over, Nanak and his friends with Mardana, the rebeck player, being chief of them withdrew to some neighbouring solitude and there spent their time in singing and prayer."

How could a person with deep yearning for the Almighty confine himself to servitude ? Nanak resigned his job and distributed all his belongings to the poor and joined the ascetic order. He retreated to a forest to meditate. Mardana followed him like a shadow in all his pilgrimages. He too, like his Guru was well versed in music and both spent fine musical moments throughout their long and hazardous journey. The journey covered quite long distances. Throughout these historic journeys, the Guru would mix with the masses and talk to them about the existence of the Almighty. Sometimes he stayed with ordinary people. It is said that at Syyidpur (Gujranwala) he stayed in the house of an ordinary carpenter, Lalo. It was here that people came to know, for the first time, about the challenge of the Guru to the old order of casteism and superstitions.

"The Brahmins and pilgrims were making offerings of water with their faces turned towards the east. Nanak went amongst them and taking large handfuls of water, threw them in the direction of the west. The Brahmins were surprised and asked Nanak as to what he meant. Nanak asked in return "what is your object please ?" They replied, "We are making offerings to our departed souls." Nanak replied, "My village is situated in the west. So I throw water towards the west. If your handfuls of water can reach the departed souls why not mine reach the fields lying only some ten miles off ?"

Guru Nanak covered on foot the most sacred pilgrimage centres of the land namely Kurukshetra, Haridwar, Brindaban and Varanasi. He challenged the supremacy of the different Brahmins. Some of them subsequently became his followers. From Varanasi he went to Puri and from Puri to Ceylon (Sri Lanka). The Guru spent more than twelve years on pilgrimages and deep meditation. Soon he returned to Talwandi. He visited also the holy Mecca and some other countries in the west.

Meanwhile the news of Babar's invasion spread. Both Nanak and Mardana were imprisoned and put under the charge of one Mir Khan, an official in Babar's army. Nanak was given rigorous imprisonment. He had to carry heavy loads on head. Mardana was forced to work with broom-sticks. It was during this period that they found women being tortured by the army. The Guru has given description of this in his self-composed poems :

"They who wore beautiful dresses and the partings of whose hair were dyed with vermilion.
Have their locks now shorn with the scissors and dust is thrown upon their heads.
They who dwelt in private chambers, now they cannot find a seat in public.
Hail ! Father hail ! O Primal Being. Thy limit is not known.
Thou makest and beholdest the different phases of existence."

Guru Nanak vividly described how "when Babar's rule was proclaimed,no Pathan prince ate his food." He was imprisoned among others. For Nanak, it was not that difficult to conquer the emperor and soon the emperor came to know about the spiritual power of the saint. Babar's devastating killings had wounded the feelings of the saint and he made it known to the emperor that it was nothing less than perpetration of atrocity and torture. Babar heard about the saint's piety and demeanour in the prison cell and when he was informed that the latter wanted to meet him and lodge protest against his tyranny, he himself wanted to see the Guru. The Guru was received by Babar in his court. Nanak told Babar on his face that his behaviour with the people was much beyond description. He told him that even above the mighty emperor there was a mightier force and that was the Almighty. The saint warned the emperor against all his sins :

"The Guru's words had such a magic effect on his mind that he showed him special respect while all his courtiers saluted him. The emperor asked him to accept a present from him. The Guru replied that he wanted nothing for himself but requested that the captives of Aminabad might be released. Upon this, the emperor ordered that they should be set free and their properties restored. Babar was so pleased with the Guru that he asked him to accompany him. The Guru at first promised to remain only one day with him, but on being pressed to remain for three days, he at last consented. But he was always distressed when he looked at the plight of the prisoners. Once he was so much affected that he fell into a trance and became unconscious. Babar was alarmed and when the Guru stood up he prayed to him to be gracious to him. The Guru replied "If thou O emperor desirest kindness, set all the captives free."Babar agreed and the Guru said, "Thy empire shall remain for a long time." The emperor on this ordered that all his prisoners should be clothed with robes of honour, an action which caused the Guru much pleasure and satisfaction. When the emperor asked for instructions the Guru replied, "Deliver just judgments, revere holy men, forswear wine and gambling. The monarch who indulged in these vices shall, if he survive, bewail his misdeeds. Be merciful to the vanquished, and worship God in spirit and in truth."

The founder of the Mughal empire readily accepted the advice of Guru Nanak and followed him religiously. When Babar requested the saint to accept some thing from him as a present the Guru told him very modestly that he would accept gifts or presents only from one person and that was the Almighty. The Guru said, "There is but one Giver, the rest are beggars."

The Guru's message was like Upanishad teachings : "God," He declared, "is at once Absolute, Universal, One without a second; and also the Friend and companion of each soul. The path to Him was simple: it lay through faith and devotion. Further, all are equal; there is no high or low with God. God is accessible to the "self-righteous holy man."

Scholars have a tendency to consider Sikhism as preached by the Guru, as an echo of Buddhism. This included the translator of the epic Adi Granth Dr. A.D. Trumpp. Scholars are also inclined to think that Guru Nanak was influenced by the teachings of Christ. In fact it was not necessary for the Guru to be influenced by anyone of the earlier thoughts. He himself attained the great truth and spread the message of love out of self-realisation. In his utterances, one could see the synthesis and assimilation of the highest thoughts of the holy scriptures of the Upanishads, the Vaishnavite mystics, the renunciation as espoused in Geeta and the messages of the Buddha and Holy Christ.

About the new religion as preached and practised by the Guru Dr. Trumpp observes :

"We can distinguish a grosser and finer kind of pantheism. The grosser pantheism identifies all things with the Absolute, the universe in its various forms being considered the expansion of it. The finer pantheism on the other hand distinguishes between the

Absolute and the finite being and others frequently on theism. Though God is producing all things out of Himself and is filling all, yet He remains distinct from the creatures and is not contaminated by the Maya, as lotus in a pond of water remains distinct from the water surrounding it. The Supreme is in its essence Light, the All-Engineering Vital Power, which though diffused into all creatures, remains distinct from them, the material is re-absorbed into the Fountain of Light. In this finer shade of pantheism, creation assumes the form of emanation from the Supreme (as in the system of the Sufis); the atomic matter is either likewise considered co-eternal with the Absolute and immanent in it, becoming moulded into various distinct forms by the energising vigour of the Absolute; or the reality of matter is more or less denied so that the Divine is the only real essence in all. That an Absolute Being, thus defined, cannot be a self-conscious spirit, endowed with a free will and acting according to theological principles seems never to have struck their minds. For, after the strongest pantheistic expressions, the Supreme is again addressed as a self-conscious personality who governs all things and takes care of all creatures and with whom man endeavours to enter into personal relations. Contradictory sentences of this kind we find a great many in the Granth. To this personification of the Supreme, it is owing that intellectual and moral qualities that are frequently ascribed to Him though, strictly speaking, there is no room for them in this system. He is called very wise, acquainted with the secrets of the hearts (or the inward Governor), not deceivable, kind to His devotees, merciful, just, etc. In other places, qualities are attributed to Him which are contradictory to each other which clearly show that they are to be taken in a particular sense."

In the holy Granth Sahib which records the sayings of the Guru there are the highest thoughts which echo like the message of Upanishads. It starts with "There is but one God whose name is true, the Creator."

As the Guru was resting under a tree, one day a holy man asked him to change his position. He thought the Fakir who was a new comer to the village perhaps did not know that his legs were spreading towards the temple. Promptly the saint asked him, "Yes my dear, you tell me which side I can change my position and where I can rest my legs because I have yet to find a place where God does not exist."

Nanak said, "God is one, He is the God, not of the Hindu, not of the Mussalman, not of the Christian, but of mankind. Under whatever name He is worshipped - Jehovah, Allah or Ram - He is the one, Invisible, Eternal, Uncreated."

To Nanak knowledge of God was the most important thing. It was not for the Brahmin alone, but for all, and all have a right to seek it for themselves. The worship of God is not the exclusive privilege of the priests. It is a service in which every man has an equal right to seek it for himself.

The Guru went from place to place singing the glory of God and spreading his divine message of love through his self-composed songs which became so popular throughout the world.The compilation-Japji has been read throughout the world by millions.

A common practice by all saints of India has been to visit places of holy pilgrimages. These visits not only widen one's ideas, but the commingling with other monks, and associations with ancient thoughts generate further spiritual power. the Guru first went to Delhi, Varanasi, Gaya, Gorakhpur and Puri. He also visited the South. He visited Madras and Ceylon (Sri Lanka).

To the Guru these visits had a special meaning. "It was the call of his restless spirit to proclaim a religion that led him on his first pilgrimage. To the crowd, as to the priest and the lay man, he preached the gospel of the oneness of soul and God, and pointed out the pathway of realisation through the Name. Time and again he would insist on directing their attention to God. His appeals were remarkable for the simplicity of expression and the exquisiteness of the illustrations that drew his point home."

The Guru said, "You have come naked into the world and naked you will depart, therefore ponder, O ignorant one, on the one who hath created thee and seek him and meditate upon him."

The Guru went around proclaiming his gospel. Almost all great saints practised their spiritual concentration for just twelve years without any break. This has been the practice right from the days of Ramachandra in the Ramayana where He is described to have meditated in a forest also for *twelve* years. The Guru practised spiritual concentration for twelve years after which he returned to Punjab but refused to return home. The affectionate mother came to take her beloved son back home.

Guru Nanak would feel as if a "dark night" had befallen him. Just like the Holy Christ, the Guru would cry in agony, "Father why hast thou forsaken me?" "The Guru left Punjab to avoid his mother. He left for Srinagar to meditate in the Himalayas. Guru Nanak's eagerness for God was doubled. These pilgrimages had given Him inner light. Now he could not think of anything but God. He wrote: "I have become perplexed in my search. In the darkness I find no way. Devoted to pride, I weep in sorrow. Alas, how shall peace be obtained ?"

There was a storm in the mind of Nanak. This was the state of mind of the great Vaishnva saint Srikrishna Chaitanya who started weeping for separation from Krishna. This was exactly the condition of Sri Ramakrishna just before he had the vision of the Mother. Without great yearning of the heart one can never get the divine light. At the foot of the Himalayas Guru Nanak retired for peace. "The retirement, however, to the Himalayan solitudes was not without its bracing effect, and the sylvan surroundings went a long way towards helping him. It was here that through meeting the holy people, he was able to get his introduction to the 'True One.' Of course, he had the first flashes of the light and trances much earlier, but now it was some thing permanent that he attained to. And after his enlightenment he returned to his native place, and then proceeded to Kartarpur, and decided to start on his second pilgrimage, this time to the West."

Separation from God was painful. His mind did not rest in peace particularly after his spiritual experiment in the Himalayas.

He decided to go to west. This was pre-destined. "Nanak first went to Patan where he was again able to meet the beloved disciple of Baba Farid by name Sheikh Bahram. The latter was very happy at the meeting and was soon convinced of the attainments of Nanak, whom he complimented by remarking, "of a certainty thou hast seen God." Nanak proceeded further, passed through Baghdad, reached Mecca and then Medina. At these very shrines and mosques he fearlessly proclaimed to the assembled crowds :

"I have appeared in this world to indicate the way unto men. I have rejected all sects and only know one God, whom I recognise in the earth, the heavens and all directions."

Vehemently did he decry and denounce mere formal worship in the various sects and religions, and condemned mere rituals and ceremonials as passage and gateway to Heaven ; while to the Hindus he said:"

> "Brahma who came into the world repeating the Vedas cannot describe Thee... Shiva and countless gods and goddesses standing at thy gate praise Thee.:
> (Mecauliffe : Sikh Relgion, Vol.I p. 128)

To the Muslim he said :

> "Merely reading the scriptures does not free the mind from anxiety. If for a moment thou restrainest thy mind God will appear before thee."

The history of the new religion of the saint Guru Nanak is the story of mankind. It is the new universal message of brotherhood of mankind - Guru Nanak did not believe in any particular sect, caste or creed. He was secular to the core. Even today he is the modernest of the modern in his views and thoughts. He is relevant very much in a world of dissension and chaotic thinking as in religious arena. It is to the advantage of world peace and progress and cohesion in thinking that international platforms will benefit to spread the message of this great Master. He symbolised the unity of religions and it was a thorough synthesis of the highest ideas that India has to preach and present to the world for centuries to come. It must be recorded here that the Guru did not found any religion. It was left to his disciples to collect and coordinate his ideas and preachings and put under one school of thought which gave birth to the new religious movement, popularly known as Sikhism. There are innumerable accounts giving details of the biographical events of this great Master. Among the great western scholars who devoted their research on the Guru, the works of Cunningham (History of the Sikhs), Macauliffe (The Sikh Religion), Scot George Batley (Religion and Short History of the Sikhs 1479-1930) and Archer John Clark (The Sikhs) are only a few to mention. Research work has also been conducted at the level of the UNESCO to popularise the universal message of love as preached and practised by Guru Nanak.

Nanak was the linking bridge between two major religions of India. To Him there was no distinction between the Hindus and the Muslims. He was much above sectarian views. He was much above any narrow dogmas. He could not be bound by any particular group or groups. His doctrines assimilated the best of the prevailing systems of thought. He accepted the Hindu pantheon but relegated it to a much lower place in his religious scheme. He also accepted the Hindu doctrine of Karma and transmigration. His conception of hell and heaven, human body, soul and God were more or less the same as those of the Hindus. But Guru Nanak denied the theory of incarnation although he had respect for the prophets of all the religions. He rejected the supremacy of the Brahmins and denounced caste and untouchability. He equally denounced idolatory and ritualism. He also denied the unquestionable sanctity attached to the Vedas and the Quran.

Guru Nanak believed in one and formless God and laid great stress on the recitation of His name. His treatment of the relation between God and man is so intensely human that the formless God merges into the devotee's personal God. He gave a very high place to a meditator, i.e. Guru in his religious system. He believed in the equality and fraternity of man. He placed great emphasis on the purity of conduct. He rejected asceticism and emphasised that a householder was equal to an ascetic in the eyes of God. He regarded life on this earth as short-lived like the shadow of a passing bird; but believed that it was left to man to make it happy or miserable. His teachings place considerable emphasis on humility as a human virtue.

The Guru had miraculous power. There are many instances associated with the life of the Guru which are not only legends but historic facts. He never wanted to show this power to anybody but they were revealed in face of circumstances. In his childhood when he left learning Persian, his father Kalu got much annoyed. He wanted to fix up the son to some job. He lost all hope and rebuked him. His idea of sending the son for a clerical job with the Nawab was dashed to the ground. He assigned him the task of looking after the buffaloes. Nanak did not mind. He gladly took up the job. He was at least freed from the materialistic surroundings and could breathe free air. Under the high blue sky, the green field of his mind would look for the great artist who created this beautiful landscape. "Where is that Master Artist, my mind ?". Kalu was surprised. How did the child accept the task so easily ? He was happy. His son was at least doing some work. He was relieved to a great extent. Nanak left the buffaloes to graze themselves. He was sleeping under the shadow of a tree and got deeply absorbed in his thoughts on the unseen Master Artist. The world is very cruel. They do not allow people to think of good things even. Very soon an angry crowd surrounded him. He was surprised at their shouting. Are they hurling all these abuses on him ? At home father did not allow him to sit for a minute to concentrate. The people too, it seemed, had joined him. Nanak felt distraught, disturbed and helpless.

What had happened ?

The buffalo herds had destroyed the farms. They trod on the farm, destroyed harvest and damaged it so badly that farmers would not leave Nanak without getting compensation. The farm belonged to one Bhatti who collected a few peasants. Nanak repeatedly requested Bhatti to forget about the loss for which he shouldered the entire responsibility. He pleaded guilty and with all humility wanted to be pardoned but Bhatti and his friends would not be satisfied. The whole party ran to lodge a complaint with the feudal lord Rai Bular. The Zamindar had high regard and deep affection for Nanak. He would always try to save the child from the cruel treatment of the father. He listened to the complaint of Bhatti who also produced a number of witnesses.

Bhatti raised a hue and cry. He fell at the feet of the feudal lord and pleaded for justice. Rai Bular had no other alternative than taking up the matter. He was sad that the case went against Nanak for whom he had not only affection but also high regard. He was very much fond of his divine songs.

His position was embarrassing. He did not know what to do. He accompanied the party to the farm. He asked, "Who said the buffalo herds had damaged crops ? There is no sign of any such harm!"

The village peasants were greatly baffled. They saw with their own eyes the damage caused. Bhatti could not explain the event. Rai Bular could guess it. He was all the more convinced now that

Nanak was an incarnation of divinity and the whole event was brought about by a miracle.

There were many similar stories about his miracles. Once the Guru was passing through a place known as Syedpur. This was during the pilgrimage. The saint was showering his blessings on one and all. In Syedpur there was a pious man, Lallo. He was a poor carpenter but a deeply religious man. He was living from hand to mouth but he was keen to have Nanak as his guest. With his long yellow robe, handsome features and a glow on his face, the saint soon became quite known in the neighbourhood.

Nanak liked Lallo, the carpenter. He was living with him. Poor man could offer him only a meagre diet. But his heart was warm with divine affection and Nanak enjoyed his company. The saint did not care for the food. A good man eats to live. Others live to eat.

Malik Bhaggo was a Dewan of the Pathan Subedar. He was known for his philanthropy and pious deeds. He used to feed monks and fakirs regularly. His invitation to the monks was a standing one.

Malik Bhaggo heard the name of the new monk whom he expected every day in his community lunch. The invitation being general he did not care to extend any special one to the saint. When Bhaggo could not see Nanak in his rich community lunch, his pride was wounded. He wondered how could it be ? While all the monks, big and small, were participating in the community lunch thrown by him, how could it be that the new monk did not care to join them, even for once ? He went to the carpenter's house and found the saint surrounded by a couple of men who were fortunate enough to listen to the golden voice of the Guru. He was showering divine nectar. This rich proud man approached the saint and, more or less, on a point of explanation asked him, why he did not join his community lunch. "Is it that you do not know me ? Do you not know I am a powerful man ?"

"Yes I know you. And that is exactly the reason why I did not join you."

The Dewan got enraged. "What do you mean" ? He bellowed.

"It is very clear. I know you. I know you so well that I do not feel like touching your *Halwa Puri*. I am quite happy with the dry piece of bread from Lallo."

The rich Dewan lost his temper. The siant's words pricked his vanity.

"You mean to say you know?"

"Yes"

"But how is it ? You never saw my face."

Nanak kept quiet.His smile provoked the Dewan.

Bhaggo said, "You must explain."

Nanak called the Dewan near him and calmly told him. "You want to see why I accept Lallo as a host and not you. Alright. Please do me a favour. Get the Puri Halwa that you want to offer me."

The saint asked Lallo, the carpenter, also to get him the dry piece of bread that he normally offered him.

Then a miracle happened. The details are given in the most authentic biography of the Master, Janam Sakhi.

Guru Nanak placed Lallo's piece of dry bread side by side with Dewan's Puri Halwa. Just to teach a lesson to the arrogant rich man the saint showed his miracle. He squeezed the Halwa Puri of Dewan. Everybody saw pure red blood pouring out of hand.

The saint kept the dry bread of Lallo, the carpenter. He squeezed this too. Everybody saw pure white milk pouring out of his hand.

"So you see why I do not join your lunch."

The Dewan fell down at the feet of the Guru and asked for his blessings and forgiveness. By and by, the story got spread. Hundreds of people started thronging around the saint. So the next dawn, the Guru left Syedpur along with Balla and Mardana.

Once Nanak was passing through Batala in Punjab. Everywhere he was surrounded by so many admirers. The saint was singing in his melodious voice in glory of God. It was on the bank of river Ravi. Hundreds of devotees - Hindus, Muslims, scholars, illiterate peasants, rich and poor- were pouring in large numbers.

Here the feudal lord was one Kadoria. He was very influential and proud. He was much jealous of Nanak's tremendous popularity. He wanted to present himself before the saint and get him out of the village. Why should an outsider,that too an ordinary monk trespass his domain and become so popular, he thought. He could not simply stand it.

He got himself dressed in his battle royal robe. He got his sword hanging round the waist as usual and got saddled on a beautiful white horse.He did not forget to take with him his guards. No sooner had he advanced little than he fell down from the horse-back. He got hurt. He had to cancel his journey. After a few days he again set forth for the saint. This time too, he again fell down and astonishingly got blinded. He could not see anything. But as soon as he returned to his palace he could see everything. Kadoria did not know what to do. Every time he thought of visiting Nanak, his body started trembling. He would lose all strength and sometimes even eye sight. But strangely whenever he was returning to his palace he was feeling perfectly fit. How could it happen ?

He asked his people.

Some of them were devoted people. They had spiritual inclination. They heard about Nanak's power. Many of them had visited the saint too. So they said the accidents were taking place only because of the King's wrath for a saint.

He got terribly frightened.

He changed his mind. "Suppose I go and pay him my respects? I hope, I should better do that."

So this time he got himself saddled on a horse to got to Nanak to pay him his tribute.

Again the same event, he got blinded. He did not know what to do.

Some persons told him, "You are going to pay your tribute to a saint, sir. You must go there with all humility. You must go on foot. Only then he will bless you."

This suddenly struck Kadoria. With all humility he went to Nanak and fell at his feet.

Nanak embraced him and gave him his blessings. His words to Kadoria were gems. The feudal lord, now a completely changed man, wanted to build a new township and make it a centre of pilgrimage. He wanted to give away to the saint the whole village.

To this the saint replied, "There is only one Lord who owns all land of the world. In fact, He owns whatever things we see. He is the great creator. You are lucky that you have realised this and have come forward to make a gift of it in His holy name. You can certainly go ahead with your idea of founding a new township here. I call the new township Kartarpur. It will become the nerve centre of the new movement dedicated to the spreading of the message of love."

Very soon it became a pilgrimage. Today it is an imporant town humming with people. Nanak's family too shifted to Kartarpur.

It is also recorded that while on pilgrimage suddenly one day he decided to return to Talwandi, his village, Mardana was surprised. Nanak told him that Rai Bular the religious man, the ruler of that township was on his death-bed and was eagerly awaiting him.

Guru Nanak reached him in time.

Rai Bular, the devoted Muslim died a happy death. Prophecy had come true. The tiny little child of his village had by now become a spiritual leader of the whole area and was respected by innumerable persons of all faiths. He breathed his last in the presence of the great saint.

Mardana was stunned. Here was the man who walked miles after miles without break, without food, without sleep just to meet his friend on his death-bed. All the friends and relations were crying. Not a drop of tear was shed by the saint. How was that? Much later Mardana put him this question.

The Guru told him, "Rai Bular was a good man. He was religious and honest. His soul must be resting in peace. There is nothing to feel sorry for his departure. Death is the main gate of life. Man's soul starts a fresh journey through it."

Nothing in this world perishes. They only undergo a change.

Man gets his place according to his work. It does not depend on rituals. It does not depend on pretentious religious activities. The Guru said :

> "Yoga does not consist of putting on the garment of rags nor in rubbing ashes on the body and in carrying a staff. Neither does it consist of shaving the head or shouting through the bugle or conch.
>
> He who has the collyrium of wisdom applied to his eyes sees the Lord in all.
>
> He sees Him who sees the one in all."

The Guru gave a practical shape to the ideas of the Bhakti Movement by coming in close contact with the masses. He undertook long journeys. Throughout his pilgrimges he had been spreading the message of love and castelessness. He did not advocate idolatory either.

The advent of Islam had infused new thoughts in Indian philosophy. The Sufis had definitely contributed much to this new great movement.

The liberal outlook of the saint held him to accept the best of contemporary thoughts. Ramanand's influence was already there. Kabir's immortal songs had been on the lips of people. Nanak, with his catholicity of mind and a wider vision of divine outlook included and welcomed the ideas of Ramananda and Kabir. He presented them too before his disciples. In this connection a learned historian observes :"Two points, however, deserve consideration in this connection. First, Guru Nanak must have absorbed fresh ideas in the course of his travels in different parts of India; the world which he saw had advanced to some extent along the liberal track laid by Ramananda. Secondly, Ramananda and his followers - especially Kabir - certainly played a recognised role in Sikh religious tradition. This is proved by the inclusion of their hymns in the Adi granth. Only one hymn attributed to Ramananda has found place in the Holy Book, but it has a typical affinity with the teachings of the Sikh Gurus."

There is no doubt that Guru Nanak laid the first brick of casteless society in modern India. In the social structure based on four castes, the first symptom was always revealed in religious practices. Although introduced on a scientific basis of division of labour, the system got degenerated and thoroughly mutilated. Nanak took up the challenge. Spiritual life was open to all irrespective of castes. Ramanuja had reserved spiritual bliss for the first three castes: "Not for Shudra is the grace of God available in this life. By dutiful conduct he may work his way up to another birth in which he may be admitted to the study of the Vedas which is indispensable for the saving knowledge." Guru Nanak recognised no such restriction based on birth. In his view every man, irrespective of his position in the caste hierarchy was eligible for salvation; those who took shelter in God were equals.

The most outstanding contribution of the Guru was his laying the foundation towards building a classless society. Judging from the influence of social set up and the centuries-old traditional conventions with its deep roots in the social structure, one must realise that the task was not an easy one. It was a stupendous one.

It was also a great challenge. It was a social revolution. The Guru had achieved it.

This most important aspect of the Guru's message has been recorded in Indian history. An eminent historian has recorded, "Much more important than external influence was his basic spiritual approach towards the problems of human life. Guru Nanak was not a social reformer in the ordinary sense of the term. He did not aim directly and specifically at removal of social injustice. His purpose was to lay down a track for man's spiritual journey. For admission to that track no social qualifications, no high rank in the social hierarchy would be needed; a craving for spiritual bliss would be the only passport. For pursuing that track it would be necessary for man to drop his inherited social prejudices. Such a spiritual venture would in itself be a social revolution. And there could be no social revolution in India without considerable erosion - if not total elimination - of the caste system which crippled human dignity and formed a dyke against spiritual regeneration."

This was not a new point of discovery. The earlier saints had already noted it. The Guru laid the foundation strongly. Bhai Gurdas, the eminent Sikh saint had emphatically observed: "Guru Nanak had reduced the four castes into one." If we take this statement in a literal sense it would imply liberalisation of traditional restrictions on prohibition of inter-caste marriage and of eating in common. There are difficulties in the way of accepting the proposition that such a society actually emerged in Guru Nanak's lifetime. If the four castes had really been reduced into one in the days of Guru Nanak, some of the reforms of Guru Gobind Singh would hardly have been necessary. He said, "Let men of the four castes receive my contempt for one another." It would appear that only those who received his baptism would be liberated from caste prejudices. Cunningham wrote, "Govind Singh abolished caste rather by implication than by a direct enactment." If Forster's statement has to be believed, the tenth Guru's injunction ceased to be effective in the eighties of the 18th century. He wrote that "the Sikhs formed matrimonial connections only within their respective tribes." These could be intellectual discourses. There was no doubt that Guru Nanak paved the way for removing casteism.

A practical demonstration of founding a classless and casteless

Social order was the introduction of Langar. Much before the popular commune system got introduced it was the Sikh Guru who popularised the system of Free Kitchen. He championed the cause of the common man. He knew their suffering. He himself hailed from such a family. The new system of Langar was introduced to foster unity among them, to break the strangle hold caste system and serve the rich and the poor from a common kitchen. "According to the general accepted tradition it was set on foot by Guru Nanak and expanded by his immediate successor, Guru Angad and Guru Nanak's teachings - denunciation of asceticism and importance of dan. Guru Nanak said, "He who eats what he has earned by his own labour and gives some (to other), Nanak, he it is who knows the true way." Apart from the religious aspect, both these points strengthened the trends towards the development of a new social structure. What we call dignity of labour was promoted and the individual's responsibility of contributing to social welfare emphasised. Moreover, it was through the system of dan that the Langar system developed. All those who came to take their food in the Langar had to take it together, irrespective of caste or creed. It was a direct blow to the caste system. It was also a direct incentive to promotion of fraternity and social solidarity. One could see how ideas propounded by Guru Nanak, primarily from the spiritual point of view, contributed to later social reform. The dynasty of the ruling Lodis was declining. Religious life had already been neglected by people. There was no importance attached to moral values. Corruption and bribery were quite rampant. It was at this point/period of time that the Guru emphasised on moral values, particularly on sympathy, piety and justice.

One social evil, caused directly by the weakness of the Lodi regime and indirectly by the decay of religion, was the widespread practice of bribery. Guru Nanak observed :

> "Compassion is not exercised by merely beholding a suitor
> There is no one who receiveth or giveth not bribes.
> The King dispenseth justice when his palm is filled."

The Guru was much in advance of his time in his thoughts. He was a friend, philosopher and guide of the poor and the downtrodden. He was a socialist to the core. He was a practical saintly philosopher. Much before the introduction of the 'earn your bread' policy enunciated by modern scholars, the Guru insisted one must not be dependent on anybody. "Kings are butchers", he said publicly. This was quite natural as in an age when, as the Guru said, "Kings are butchers." By drawing pointed attention to this evil practice, Guru Nanak showed how he shared the common man's feelings and grievances, for it was the common man on whom this practice must have pressed very hard. He could suggest no direct remedy, but he tried to strike at the very root of the evil by saying: "He who eats what he has earned by his own labour... he it is who knows the true way."

For the new movement of social equality all the saints of the Bhakti Movement worked hand in hand. In fact, it will not be proper to single out any one of them. They did it as a team. They did not differentiate among themselves. The real aim was to raise the moral values in the life of the common people. A common man greeted this happy symphony. It has been recorded that "Ramanuja, however, did not go far enough. It was Ramananda, an adherent to the Ramanuja school, who offered more generous recognition to the spirit of the age. He admitted to his sect disciples from all castes, even from Muslims, and called them, 'the liberated.' As a systematic expounder and propagator of the Bhakti cult he deemed forms of adoration as superfluous, and held that the supreme reward of devotion was to be obtained by incessantly uttering God's name." The simplification of worship and the liberalisation of the tradational caste rules were Ramananda's most important contribution to the solution of the religious problems of his day. He had closer contact with Islam than Ramanuja. "At Benaras", observes Mecauliffe, "he came in contact with 'learned Mussalmans". The influence of Islam was probably not an unimportant factor in the development of his ideas."

Guru Nanak gave practical shape to the Bhakti Movement irrespective of the earlier saints. It would be futile to infer a surmise about indebtedness, of one saint to the other. It would be purely academic and redundant. They were in fact, complementary to each other.

Guru Nanak was equally respected by Hindus and Muslims. His most trusted disciple who accompanied him throughout his journeys on pilgrimages, was Mardana a devoted Muslim. Hindu and Islam religions both were in India were in a decaying condition. Hindu religious leaders lost their grip on moral values. Similarly the Muslims were indifferent to religion. The rulers were Muslims. They were more interested in collecting funds through bribes and corrupt practices than practising their religion. It was said, once the saint was criticising the lack of moral values of social leaders and he was summoned by Kazi, a representative of the ruler. When he asked him about his religion, Nanak said, he was neither Hindu nor a Muslim. The Kazi was surprised. However to test him, he invited him to join in Namaz. At prayer time the saint did not join him. Later on when the Kazi asked him the reason, Nanak said, "How could I join you ? You were not thinking of God. You were thinking of the earthly things only." He was only calculating loss and gain in his trade. The Kazi had to agree. The saint's readings were correct.

Guru Nanak never believed in the extraneous formalities or rituals. An honest heart was the dwelling place of God. So an honest person need not necessarily be bound by rituals. Guru Nanak said, "A Sadhu possesses goodness even if he does not bathe and a thief, even if he bathes, remains a thief."

It would be seen "The keynote of the religious problems of Guru Nanak's age was most strikingly expressed in the famous pronouncement attributed to him." "There was the product," as Teja Singh says, "of the very peculiar turn of their mind, with which they would take those things as ends in themselves which were originally intended only as means." In other words, rituals were mixed up and confused with religion.

The saint saved the disciples from the time-old orthodox rituals. "Guru Nanak's condemnation of the traditional rituals was practically unqualified. He recognised that 'some little honour' might be obtained through the performance of pilgrimage, austerities, mercy, and alms-giving on general and special occasions! But the far better method of washing off impurity was to "hear", obey and love God." In general, he prescribed God's name as "the best thing' in this Kali age.

The saint wanted his followers to avoid idolatory. Great reformers of renaissance movement like Raja Ram Mohan Roy, Keshab

Chandra Sen, Ishwar Chandra Vidya Sagar, Swami Dayanand Saraswati followed this precept later. Much before these great leaders, Guru Nanak said, "Blind and dumb (they i.e. the Hindus) walk in pitch darkness, worshipping this ridiculous stone which they have set up. It sinks, so how can it carry you across (the ocean of existence)?"

On the futility of the current ascetic practices the Guru observed, "He who sings songs about God without understanding them; who converts his house into a mosque in order to satisfy his hunger; who, being unemployed, has his ears pierced (so that he can beg as a yogi); who becomes a faqir and abandons his caste; who is called a Guru or pir but who goes around begging, never fall at the feet of such a person."

Guru Nanak was an incarnation of humility. It is indeed interesting to find that all saints of India had surrendered themselves completely to the Almighty and thought it fit to pray to the universal Father to give them strength to reach the final goal. Nanak sang in a similar vein. In his famous hymns :

Sab abagun nahi gun koi
Kiun Kar Kant milawa hoi
Na mai rup na banke naina
Na kul dhang na mithe baina

The saint noted : "I am full of faults in every way. How shall I gain my Lord?"

In a beautiful hymn included in Guru Granth Sahib, the enlightened Guru exalted "Try to get the Almighty in your heart. The Lord dwells in one's heart."

The Guru sang :

> Dwell within thyself (seek Him not outside). Drink nectar and exchange it not for poison.
>
> Be a true servant of the Lord. This teaching has been imparted to me by my Guru.
>
> Many take recourse to wisdom and contemplation, and want to circumscribe the Lord.

Mere religious sittings or pretentious prayers do not help any one. That was the message of all the saviours of mankind. Nanak too insisted that without yearning for God, none can obtain that heavenly nectar. One has to make one's mind keen to Lord as lotus loves water.

Ray man aisi Hari sewn prit kar
Jaise jal Kamaleh
Lahari nal pachharaye bhi
Bigasai asaneha

The deep significance of the song would touch any ordinary human heart. The relation between man and God has been explained so clearly in a simple style by the saint.

Love the Lord as the lotus loves the water,
Even though with its waves the lotus is lashed, yet it does not abandon its Love, instead blooms all the more.

The original lines of Guru Nanak say

Chakabi nainan neend nahi chahe
  Bin pir neend na pae
Sur charai piu dekhai nainan
  Nib nib lagai pai
Piu bhavai prem sakhai
  Tis ghari nahi jagajiva
Aisi pyas tisai.

Even as poems, they are taken as gems. They point out the highest thoughts of Indian philosophy in the simplest style. And for the first time, the ordinary people of the land could taste the heavenly nectar of that immortal message of India through the voices of these saints. Guru Nanak was among the foremost ones. He represents the highest thoughts of India and Nanak's voice of Love reflected the voice of whole of India. He belongs to the whole world when, through his divine ecstacy, the Guru sang:

Hari bin kium jeevai ray bhai
Jai Jagadish tera jas jachai
Mai Hari bin rahia na jai.

Guru Nanak could not bear the pangs of separation from God. He could not also live in separation from that God Almighty who has been worshipped by the millions. Hari had been the subject of adoration of all Indian saints.

Guru Nanak sang in this immortal song:

> O Lord! I cannot live away in separation from Thee any longer,
> I survive only by reciting and singing of Thy exploits.
> O Lord! The night in remembrance and waiting for Thee is past,
> Ye knoweth the thirst of my soul, the ache of my heart,
> Therefore come and save me.

Constant prayer was a habit of all the saints. They all have been pleading that men should not waste even a minute in idle gossip or sleep or enjoyment. Each life has a purpose in this universe. And that is concentration of mind on God. Nanak cautioned us against such a life that has not been dedicated to God. The Guru said in Guru Granth Sahib :

> Alack ! What a pity, the night in sleep ye passed away and the day in feeding the body.
> Costly as a rich diamond was your life which ye
> frittered away as a broken shell.
> Remember therefore that the Lord, thy Creator and
> Creator of the world knows what is best.
> All greatness falls to the lot of one on whom He confers it.
> So said Nanak.

It has been the spirit of highest Indian thoughts and traditions that all great saints of the land prescribed the same nectar, sermon of complete surrender to God Almighty. "God runs this universe. We are mere instruments." That was also the message of the Holy Christ. Nanak observed :

> I am a handmaiden of my Lord,
> By killing my ego I have gained my Lord,
> My Lord is the Light effulgent.

The Guru's songs were so penetrating and his melodious voice so enchanting because the saint was an Enlightened soul. He definitely had vision. If only one cares to collect together the descriptions of the Almigty by some great saints of the world one would be convinced of a supramental great power which can be seen and the presence felt in one's own life time. The description of the Almighty has been the same. People may worship Him in different forms. In fact that great fountain source of all power has no shape, no image. It is a great flood of soft light like a million tube lights. Only the fortunate few can see that. Guru Nanak has given a vivid description of his vision.

The lotus-bud of the heart blooms in full. The eyes are witnesses of the flood of light. The Great *Guru* sang in ecstasy.

Sab mahi jyoti, jyoti hai soi
Tiadoi chanan sabha mahi chanan hoi
Gursathi jyoti pargat hoi
Jo tisu bhavai su arati hoi

Nanak, the enlightened, saw for himself the flood of light. It has been the source of all lights. The sun, the moon, the stars all derive their light from it. The Guru is the real Guide and, only at His (Guru's) feet and at His (Guru's) mercy one can see that light. Oh Master (Guru), I have come to know, I have realised whatever pleases you,whatever brings joy to you is your arati. The Enlightened one was ordained by the merciful God to carry the message of Love. He was assured that God would be there dwelling all the time in his heart.

Truth is universal. The paths to that truth may be many but great minds coincide. Revealed Truth, realised Truth is described in the same way. Chaitanya Mahaprabhu said ,"In the Kaliyug there is no other way to get salvation than only uttering the holy name of God." The biographer of Chaitanya record this emphatically; for more than five centuries the followers of Mahaprabhu have been practising the same. And what a coincidence! Guru Nanak points out again and again that "the Name is the Teacher, and the Name is the only pathway. There is no other road but the Name, and that is the only door for getting salvation, in this Kaliyug." He insisted, this must be closely followed with deep devotion. To Guru Nanak "the Name and the Master (Satguru) were one and he made no distinction between the two."

To quote the nectar words of the Guru, "For a diseased world the remedy is the Name." Scholars have given different interpretations to this. "To this all-important word "Name" different meanings were attached in different contexts. Sometimes it meant "God Himself", sometimes "God as revealed", and sometimes the word (Shabad). No one could be imbued with the true love of the 'Name' without instruction from the 'Guru'. None has realised God without the true Guru; without the true Guru, none." Once again Guru is God; the Guru is the voice of God; and the Guru is the Word, the Truth of God." The influence of Karma was recognised so far as it determined a favourable or unfavourable birth; but the principal determining factor in man's quest for salvation was the divine grace (Mehr): "It is through grace that the door of salvation is found." One may accept the theory of a learned historian who noted, "One who condemned conventional rituals so unreservedly as Guru Nanak could not be expected to prescribe complicated religious ceremonies for his followers. He recommended Nam Japan or 'repetition of the Name' and Nam Simran or 'remembering the Name'. In neither case was it to be mere mechanical process. There was to be asceticism; one should eat what one had earned by one's own labour and give some to others. In this recommendation for 'giving some to others' we have the origin of the practice of 'dan'. Whether 'Snan', in the sense of bathing as cleansing and purifying act, formed part of Guru Nanak's injunctions is not quite clear, although Bhai Gurdas seems to imply that Nam, Dan and Snan stand for the entire message delivered by Guru Nanak for the uplift of mankind."

It was in autumn 1538 (October) that before the Hindu and Muslim followers Guru Nanak gave His last sermon.

"Let the Hindus put flowers on my right and Muslims on my left underneath my sheet. Whose flowers were found fresh in the morning, may dispose of the body." When the sheet was removed the next morning the body had disappeared and both sets of flowers were smiling and the withered acacia tree had blossomed forth to offer its homage to the great saint.

Guru Nanak was not only the founder of the Sikh religion, he gave the whole of India a social order with a new revolutionary turn. He was a great visionary who could visualise much ahead the dream of founding a socialistic pattern of casteless, classless society. His principle of "earn your own bread" much before Thoreau, has inspired a spirited race of Sikhs who are perhaps the most industrious, hardworking and diligent people in the world. Loyal to the Guru, the Sikhs never depend on anybody's mercy. They never lean on anybody. There is no country in the world where Sikhs are not found. And wherever there are Sikhs there must be Gurudwaras. Today, Guru Nanak's message is having its echo reverberating throughout the world. Wahe Guru! Victory to the

Guru! His greatest contribution to the whole world has been the spread of the Holy Name. "Without His priceless Name there is no release from bondage and when the sound of His Name fills the heart, all bliss and salvation is its reward."

Rabindranath Tagore described Guru Nanak as "the teacher of mankind."

Guru Nanak Devji was a symbol of communal harmony. His greatest message to the world is universal brotherhood of man. Nanak outright rejected all sects. He could, in his great vision, think of a secular land where people should worship only one God. "I have appeared in this world to indicate the way up to men. I have rejected all sects and only know one God, whom I recognise in the earth, the heavens and all directions."

Nanak was one of the forerunners of the great Bhakti Movement. He decried ritualistic orthodox formal worship in various sects and religions.

Nanak was an enlightened soul. He had divine intuitions. He could visualise a stage of supramental state of mind, a state of Sachchidananda.

Guru Nanak arose to liberate the people from narrowness of their creed. He proclaimed that religion was not locked up in books, however sacred. He taught Hindus and Muslims to regard each other as brothers. He proclaimed the equality of men and women. He attacked the notion that God dwelt in the cooking pot, and instituted the practice of Langar, free kitchen where people of all castes and religions would take their food together.

The age in which Guru Nanak lived and preached was a period of weak but oppressive Muslim rule, frequented by Mongol invasions with all incidents of mass killings, carnage, pillage and persecution.

It was also a period of intense mental and intellectual fermentation. Islam and Sufism, which enjoyed the support and patronage of the state were making strides, and the beliefs and practices which were associated with them, one and formless God, equality and brotherhood of man, value of prayer, ungodliness of idols etc. - were no more confined within their fold.

Guru Nanak's doctrines, as was natural, were greatly influenced by the ideas and institutions prevailing at that time. He assimilated the best elements from all the religions he came into contact with.

He believed in one and formless God and laid great stress on the recitation of His Name. His description of the relation between God and man is clothed in the language of human love so much so that the formless God has virtually become the devotee's personal God. He gave a very high place to mediator i.e. Guru, in his religious system. He believed in the equality and fraternity of man. In the Holy Guru Granth the saint has given the highest exposition of secularism.

Guru Nanak left a deep impact on Indian culture and philosophy, as reflected in the writings and utterings of great Indian savants, saints and poets of national status. He was an incarnation of humility.

Who is an ideal Man? The great Guru found no difference between man and man. He defined an ideal man as, "He who is true, is contented, who is kind to everyone, and is devoid of greed and hatred, is not bigoted, has no evil desire, has controlled his self, knows right from wrong and has placed himself physically as well as spiritually at the disposal of God and who has cultivated the habit of following His dictates, such a balanced man has become worthy of being the Guru's disciple."

Nanak's catholicity and faith in universal brotherhood was best exemplified in his nominating not his own son, but one of chosen disciples, Lehna, whom he named as Angad as the second exalted and revered Guru of Sikhs.

5

Guru Angad Dev
Paragon of Selfless Service

To Guru Angad goes the credit of starting collection and compilation of the immortal hymns by Guru Nanak. We should be grateful to this selfless saint for his untiring zeal in collecting the nectar of messages from the Guru. As a direct result of this literary venture, India became richer in another sphere; that was the genesis of a sacred script - the Punjabi language, also known as Gurmukhi. The Gurmukhi alphabet owe their origin to Guru Angad. It came to be so known because in this holy language the Guru had given his message of God realisation and that which came from the mouth of the Guru is called reverentially Gurmukhi.

According to the philosophy of Nanak "The Guru was the central unifying personality and in spite of changes in succession was held to be identical with his predecessors." This has been exactly what Guru Parampara thoughts of some of the Hindu sects believed and practised. Although the head of the organisation came to be replaced by a new one, due to death or some other reasons, the respect and devotion to the head was as much as to the Guru Maharaj.

To the Sikhs, the Guru is as much respected as Nanak himself. In the coronation ode of Satta and Balwand, the real respect that a Guru commands is described :

> Guru Nanak proclaimed the accession of Lehna as a reward for service. He had the same light, the same method; the Master merely changed his body. The wise being, Guru Nanak, descended into the form of Amar Das. 'Thou Ram Das, art Nanak, thou art Lehna, thou art Amar Das. The human race comes and goes, but thou, O Arjan, art ever new and whole..

During the days of the Sixth Guru, Mohsin Fani wrote about the Sikhs in the Dabistan "Their belief is that all the Gurus are identical with Nanak." Guru Govind Singh wrote on the subject, "All take them as different from one another; very few recognise them as one in spirit. But only those realise perfection who do recognise them as one."

It should be specially remembered that all Gurus signed as Nanak. It has been not only that the followers looked to them as their spiritual head, more importantly, the Guru identified himself completely with Guru Nanak. To him, for all practical purposes he had no separate individuality. In mind, spirit and thought he has been Nanak.

Lehna was born in a small village in Punjab - Matedi Sarai—in the district of Ferozepur in 1504 AD. Both father Pheru and mother Daya Kaur were known for their deep religious leanings and kindness. They came from a business community and were respected for their honesty and integrity. Particularly, mother Daya Kaur was an incarnation of austerity and simplicity. She would spend all the time in religious pursuits, fasting and serving the needy and the poor. When Lehna was born, Daya Kaur had an intuition that a great soul had come on earth.

Hardly had Lehna completed his elementary education in the village school, when his father engaged the young boy in family business. Gradually the boy made good progress and the parents got him married to a beautiful peasant girl Khibi. Khibi was a devoted wife. Lehna and Khibi had two sons - Dasu and Datu. The village was the target of alien attack, the Mughals and Baluch armies rampaged the village and Lehna had to leave his native village with the family. He reached Khadur, a little village in Amritsar. It was an altogether new environment and Lehna started his household affair right from scratch. The village however had a special charm for Lehna. It was most suitable for spiritual pursuit. It seemed there was a real touch of nature that made him eager to explore the universal Truth -the realisation of inner divine light through meditation. The whole village was a pious family devoted to Devi Jwalamukhi whose temple was not far from the village. Every year Lehna would visit the temple during the autumn festival. He was a great devotee of the Almighty Mother and would reach the temple with a couple of village neighbours. He would dance in ecstasy in front of the Mother. He was already well known as a kind person, pious to the core and the whole neighbourhood respected him as a spiritual man.

As usual, Lehna used to get up early in the morning and would offer his prayer. One day it so happend that he heard a few lines of a song by neighbour Jodha. Jodha was singing the song with a spirit of complete abandon to God and Lehna felt deeply attracted by its soul stirring message. He felt as if the whole song was an address to him. He immediately rushed to Jodha and asked him who was the lucky poet to have composed such a beautiful song. He must have been an enlightened soul otherwise one could not ever pour out such a divine nectar. The heavenly melody was an eye-opener for the pious man, who could compose such divine song with such deep feeling?

Hari bin pew jeeban nay bhai
Jai Jagadish tera jas jachi mai Hari bin rahana na jai
Hari ki pyas payasi Kamini dekhow rain sabai.
Sridhara Nath mera man lina Prabha janoi peer parai.
Ganta Sarir peer hai Hari bin, Guru sabdi Hari pai
Hohu dayal kripa karo Hari jeeba Hari sew rahan Samai.
Aisi rabata rabahu man merey Hari charana chit lai
Bisam bhoye guna gaye monohara nirabhon sahaj samai
Hridaya nama sada dhana michhola ghatay na kimata pai,
Bin nabai sah koi niradhana Satguru bujh byjhai
Pritama pran bhoye suno sujani dutmyhay bis khai
Jab ki upaji tab ki taisi ranga bhoi man bhai
Sahaja sammadhi sada liba Hari siba jeelyan Hari guna gai,
Guru Kai sabda rata bairagi nija ghar tadi lai.
Shudha ras nama maharas mitha nija ghar tatgusain.
Tanha man janba hi toi rakhia oisi Guru moti pai.

Sanaka samadi Brahmadi Indradika Bhakti rate bana ai
Nanak Hari binu ghani na jiban Hari ka nam badhai."

The divine melody of the song was still ringing the whole area. The little heart of Lehna was throbbing. He could not express his real feelings. It took him sometime to reach the neighbour and asked him "My dear Jodha, tell me really where did you get this heavenly nectar ?"Unknowingly the seed of divine search was sown. The great unknown was harping a tune in the heart of the pure and enjoying his reaction to it. Lehna was impatient to know about Truth. Jodha repeated the song :

O Lord! I cannot live away in separation
from Thee any longer,
I survive only by reciting and singing of Thy exploits.
O Lord ! the night in remembrance and waiting for Thee is past,
Ye know the thirst of my soul, the ache of my hert,
therefore come and save me.
If the Guru lends me his tender hand and the
Lord showers His grace sweetly, I shall discard my ego and attain my Oneness with Him.
Lead a humble life and pass it in His remembrance
and His contemplation.
If you pass your hours and days singing praise of Him,
ye shall merge and lose your separate identity-
consciousness will come.
His name is the greatest treasure and my pure heart always preserves it,
The Guru confers the Name. Without the Name one remains a beggar.
O, my friend, my life is a veritable sacrifice to Him.
I offer it to him as also all traits of mine,
I am lost in singing of His praises and pass my time in contemplating on Him.
The Guru having imparted the word,
My household is turned into a solitude.
I am ever immersed in its heavenly nectar.
The purest and the sweetest essence is the Name which takes thee back to the eternal home.

The Guru gave me this wisdom.
Which got me a glimpse of Him
And dwelling in His eternal abode.
Only through devotion to Him
Sanak, Sanandan, Brahma and Indra have
acquired great powers.
Very great and all powerful is Name.
I cannot live without its shelter
Even for a moment, so says Nanak.

"Who is this great man who is calling Lehna so eagerly?" He felt like meeting the composer of this song immediately. In his heart of hearts Lehna felt this was a song meant only for him.He felt it was a warning to him too. Why was he not searching his Guru? Was he not wasting all his precious time all these days ? How was it that the song expressed exactly the feelings of his heart?

"Pray dear Jodha, tell me where did you get this nectar ?"

Jodha was lucky fellow. And Lehna did not know as yet that he was luckier still.

"I have learnt this song at the feet of my great Master. He has taught me this song personally. He is my spiritual preceptor Sadguru Nanak - the divine messenger whc has come to save mankind. He is my saviour."

For a moment Lehna envied Jodha. "So this lucky person has got his Sadguru. He is fortunate enough to have found his spiritual pathfinder. What about him? Is he so unfortunate and neglected that the divine light did not touch him ? Is he not worthy of the kind showering of blessings of the Lord?"

The very name Nanak sent a thrilling sensation through Lehna. There was an electric current like wave coursing through his whole body. The song had already made him mad. The name has now made him almost fall in to an ecstatic state.

"I must see him and just now. I have wasted a lot of time. I cannot afford to do it any more. You perhaps cannot appreciate my mental agony. I am not in a position to explain that. For heaven's sake, kindly lead me to him. Somehow I feel he too is eagerly waiting for me, otherwise why this song would stir my mind ?"

"My Good heavens, you had been so many times to Jwalamukhi.

That temple of the holy mother attracts you so much. Did you not happen to pass through Kartarpur? For it is only in Kartarpur that my beloved Guru resides with his happy disciples. You must be paying a visit to the holy temple in autumn next. Why not visit my Master too?"

Lehna was exceedingly happy. He must immediately start for the pilgrimage. As usual he called all his colleagues who should accompany him to Jwalamukhi temple. "Listen dear, this time our pilgrimage has a special attraction. On the bank of the river Ravi, resides a great spiritual pathfinder, a saint of the age. That is in the village Kartarpur.He is an enlightened saint. This time our programme includes a visit to the saint. We must enrich our spiritual experience by his divine guidance. His very company will give us great inspiration. Only after paying our tributes to the saint, we shall reach the Jawalamukhi temple."

All readily agreed.

The whole party reached Kartarpur. The saint was singing a melodious song:

> Antari basoi na bahari jai
> Amrita chhori kahay bishu khai

"Does he know Lehna has arrived ? Is he telling this to Lehna only? How is it that, everytime he listens to Nanak's songs, he feels they are all addressed only to him? How is it that they reflect the replies to his inner quests ?"

Lehna was setting himself for pilgrimages. He wanted to learn divine blessings by undertaking long pilgrimages. Even now, at the moment, he was at the temple of great saint to earn divine blessings. He was searching the real path. The answer came from the saint :

> Dwell within thyself
> Seek Him not outside
> Drink nectar and exchange it not for poison.

Guru Nanak continued his song -

> Be a true servant of the Lord
> This teaching has been imparted by my Guru.
> Many take recourse to wisdom and contemplation
> They want to circumscribe the Lord

I, however, by serving Him, win Him over
He dwells in everything and comprises all.

Lehna was spell bound. How could the Guru know about his queries ? How was it that he was replying to his eternal quest so easily, so softly, so spontaneously and so affectionately?

"He must be an Antaryami. He must show him the right way."- Lehna felt thrilled. "He has reached his goal. What a magnetic personality! What a blissful beaming face ! What a symbol of compassion, love and piety" Lehna felt he was face to face with God Almighty. What a serene calm face!" He felt like falling at his feet. That must have been the reason why his heart was yearning to come here. The words of the saint pierced into his heart and stirred the whole soul. He felt some invisible power was dragging him to the path he was trying to trace all these years. Ever since the musical melody entered his ears he felt he met the pathfinder in person. He felt a soothing touch, a soft and affectionate hand on his head and this had a tremendously cooling effect on his whole mind.

Lehna forgot all his colleagues. He forgot the huge crowd that assembled to listen to the nectar messages of the holy man. His whole mind left for an unseen world flying over the clouds in the sky and much above the horizon of earth and space. He was in a blissful state of mind. He did not know for how long he was in this trance. Suddenly he felt an affectionate touch. It was the saint himself. What a fountain of light! What a spring of joy and light! Lehna was overwhelmed with emotions. He simply fell at his feet.

"My Lord, my sweet heart, you have to give me shelter at your feet. I have been spending sleepless nights in search of a pathfinder. My heart was bleeding all these months and years. Now that I am lucky to meet you, I am not leaving you. You have to show me the way."

"My son, you are on a pilgrimge. You are on your way to the temple of Devi at Jwalamukhi. Better go there now. On your way back come here. We shall have some discussion quietly."

Discussions! What discussions ? He did not need any discussions. He did not need any pilgrimage. He wanted only the guidance of the saint. He has got his holy company. He did not aspire for anything else. He had got the touchstone. Why should he care for gold? Nothing could allure him now.

Lehna took leave of all his fellow colleagues. He asked them to go ahead. They left for Jwalamukhi, the temple of Devi. Lehna gave them *payals* (ghoongrus) with which he used to dance every year in autumn during the Navaratra festival in the temple. This will be a departure from the usual routine after a long time.

Lehna stayed at Kartarpur. Lehna's sudden change was reported to his family members in due course. He was requested to return home. Even the Guru who was an extremely kind saint wanted Lehna to return home. But Lehna would not listen to anybody, not even to Guru Nanak. He left his deity, he left his family and he left his family business.

Giving some details of the incident Khushwant Singh writes :

> "Lehna had been a devout Hindu before he met Nanak. At the very first meeting he fell under the spell of the Guru's words and abandoned the worship of his Gods and his business, to devote himself to the services of the Sikh community at Kartarpur.Twice Nanak persuaded him to return to his family at Khadur, but both times he came back. His devotion convinced the Guru that Lehna would make a better leader than either of his own sons. An additional factor in preferring Lehna was the fact that he had a sizeable following of his own which he was gradually bringing into the Sikh fold. To forestall subsequent opposition from his sons, Nanak expressed his preference to Lehna in public : 'Thou art Angad, a part of my body."

The learned scholar also mentions that "Long before his death he (Nanak) had one of his chief disciples, Bhai Buddha, daub Angad's forehead with saffron and proclaim him as the Second Guru." (A History of the Sikhs, Vo. I, page 49).

By his hard work, complete surrender, selfless service to the organisation and undivided loyalty, Guru Angad had won the greatest affection and highest blessing of the Lord. There could be no doubt that Nanak had greater affection for Lehna than even his two sons. Some contemporary writings and songs also observe that the Guru had greater confidence in Lehna than even his own two sons.

The eldest son Sri Chand was expected to take charge of the organisation after the saint's passing away. In fact many of the disciples of Nanak had taken that decision among themselves. "They refused to accept Angad's succession and began to create difficulties. On the advice of Nanak, Angad left Kartarpur and went to lit the Guru's lamp in Khadur where his wife and children were living."

(Gurdas, Varan quoted by Khushwant Singh op cit)

While proclaiming Lehna as the Second Guru of the Sikhs, Nanak observed "He (Lehna) had the same light and the same ways. The Guru merely charged his body."

(Var, Satta and Balwand)

Nanak himself took the task of training Lehna. He would recite before him the original songs just composed in praise of the Almighty Japji and explained to him the inner meaning of the songs. The loyal devotee devoured them with rapt attention.

Guru Nanak would tell him about the endless effects of the Holy Name. Even by listening to them a person becomes elevated. They become as divine as Shiva, Brahma or Indra. Only those who know its secret power get the right path of spiritual attainment away from the mysteries of the worldly bodies. The listening to the Holy Name opened the secret of Knowledge. It acted as the key to all divine knowledge in heart in the scriptures, Smriti and the Vedas. Only the devotees know about its real significance.

(Macauliffc, The Sikh Religion, p 198)

The devotee was enchanted by the Guru's teaching. He could not think that God realisation was so easy. To him it was an uphill task and he could not dream of seeing God. Now that the Guru had shown him the way, he must get initiated. He must join the order. He was impatient. He could not wait any longer. The Guru was very much there. Why any delay now ?

He fell down at Guru Nanak's feet. The Guru lift him up and calmly told him not to worry. The right moment was almost ahead. He must get ready. Before that Lehna was to meet his family. Guru Nanak sent Lehna to his village Khadur. The saint wanted him to first settle his family. He also wanted Lehna to discuss the matter with his family members, particularly his wife. He did not like him to do anything in a hurry. Most reluctantly Lehna left for his village.

The wife, an innocent and pious lady was happy to welcome her husband back but was disappointed when she came to know the purpose of his visit. Ever since the neighbours returned and the rumour had spread that Lehna had turned a mendicant, this pious lady had been only cursing her own fate. Was she nobody? Did Lehna not care for her a bit even ? Did he not consider it his duty even to tell her about his plans? All these days she had been brooding to herself. Now, that Lehna had shown his face she was happy. Being a pious woman, she too had high regards for the holy men. When finally she heard the plan of Lehna she agreed reluctantly to his joining the order of the Guru.

Now,Lehna returned Kartarpur with redoubled zeal. She had given him her consent. He was apprehending opposition. But if God so whished who could stand in the way? After all she was also a religious type of wife. She paid equal respects to Nanak. Who in North India did not bow his head before Guru Nanak ? In the spiritual pursuits of the saints, the maximum unnoticed sacrifice had been from the wives amd, the mothers, but unfortunately, nowhere have these been recorded in the cultural history of the land.

Lehna hurried to Kartarpur. With the approval of his wife his efforts now became more vigorous. He was doubly enthusiastic about his joining the order. He was grateful to Khivi, his beloved wife.

When the cheerful Lehna reached Kartarpur only the saint's partner Sulakhani Devi was present there. Nanak had gone to the field to supervise the harvest. The entire community - lunch popularly known as Langar - depended on this harvest. So the spiritual leader was supervising the whole thing himself. His wife welcomed Lehna. She liked this devotee more than she loved her sons. In fact, by his loyalty, humility, hard work and sincerity, Lehna had become the favoured of all. Sulakhani was glad to get Lehna back. She was glad to know that Lehna's wife Khivi had no objection to his joining the order. She directed the loyal devotee to the field to meet the Master.

There he was guiding the farm as he had been guiding millions in the right path of enlightenment. Heaps of harvested crops were lying there and none was agreeing to carry the load. It was a problem for the Guru to carry the whole crop home. Was it really a problem or he wanted to test his followers? Lehna was excited. He fell at the feet of the Master. He knew, the right moment of initiation was not far now. He was eager to tell him everything in one second. He was going to pour out his heart to the idol of his heart. But what was this? Why was he so worried?

The field was muddy. The huge crops were lying in big bundles. Everybody was keen not to spoil his dress. Who would like to spoile his cloth for this menial work ?

Lehna did not stop. He at once want near the whole stock. "How many of them do you want me to carry, my Lord?" Nanak said, "as many as you can." With great difficulty Lehna carried three huge bundles of crops on his head and started walking with his Guru.

Sulakhani Devi was working at the gate of the Ashram. When she saw Lehna carrying the huge load on his head she felt sad. "How was it that of all persons, the whole work was left only to him? He has just arrived in Kartarpur on foot after a long journey. None of you could care to note that he was so tired?" It was the voice of an affectionate mother.

But what was this?

The entire dress of the devotee was coloured in saffron. That was natural saffron. The *Sherwani*, the *Kurta*, the *Pugree*, all were dyed in natural saffron? All present in the ashram precinct felt surprised.

Guru Nanak said, "Do not get upset. It is the will of God that Lehna carries the most difficult three loads on his own shoulder. This is only the beginning."

The Guru was hinting at the future responsibilities that the devotee was going to shoulder soon. They were the symbols of three most important responsibilities of the order - spiritual, material and the physical leadership.

There was no obstacle now. Lehna was initiated by Guru Nanak. He became one of the most trusted disciples of the Guru.

Lehna did not leave any stone unturned to abide by the directions of the Guru to achieve God realisation. His path of success in spiritual realm was the path through complete surrender, unselfish service and full loyalty to the Guru. He was like Hanuman to SriRamchandra, a symbol of devotion. He attained enlightenment through this path. Any direction of Guru was abided by Angad Dev as an order and he carried that to the last. Guru Angad says, "The greatest obstacle to Sadhna is ego. It always stands in the way of God-realisation. It keeps one away from God and to get rid of this ego one must serve the preceptor - the Guru, selflessly, loyally and most sincerely." He did not just preach it. He had demonstrated this through his own life and work.

The Guru's words to him were heavenly nectar. And that was why he did not like a single expression of the saint to be missed to the world.

When the Guru passed away the saint was busy in deep meditation in a hut. He was found out by a fellow disciple, Bhai Buddha, who through spiritual insight recoverd him. He meditated for six months without break and when his fellow disciples saw him they marvelled at the glow on his face. He was looking almost like Guru Nanak. It was at the request of Bhai Buddha that he took charge of the whole order after the passing away of the Guru.

ANGAD means "Of my own limb." This name was given to his favourite disciple Lehna by Guru Nanak himself who picked him up as the next head of the Sikh order. He did not choose either of his sons as his successor. Describing this incident in his "A History of the Sikhs," Khushwant Singh says: -

> "Among the disciples who attached themselves to the Guru at Kartarpur was one Lehna, a Khatri of the Trehan subcaste, who impressed Nanak by his devotion and qualities of leadership. The Guru's elder son Sri Chand had become an ascetic and Nanak disapproved of asceticism. The younger son, Lakshmi Das turned the other way and showed no interest in spiritual matters. Consequently, Nanak chose Lehna to carry on his mission, giving him the name ANGAD (of my own limb)."
>
> (A History of the Sikhs, Vol I, p 36)

Like the Guru, Angad was secular to the core, for Nanak was an embodiment of unity of thought both to the Hindus and the Muslims.

Baba Nanak sah fakir
Hindu ka guru, Musalman ka pir

He was the Guru of the Hindus and Pir of the Muslims. He was the ideal for all secular thinkers of the country. Guru Angad himself was a good composer. Sixty-two of his hymns are to be found in the Adi Granth.One of the sweetest is Akhin bajhan vekhna fin kana sunana.

The songs have been greatly influenced by the teachings of Guru Nanak with whom Guru Angad identified himself completely. Any body who listened to it will not be wrong to mistake it as a composition by Guru Nanak himself. Guru Angad Dev observed:

To see without eyes,
without ears, hear,
To walk without feet
without hands work,
To speak without a tongue -
Thus living, yet detached from life.
Oh Nanak, if you follow the word of your Master
You shall surely meet Him.

Even the signature at the end of the poem carries the name of Nañak Dev and not his own. It was perhaps because the moment a Sikh saint took over as the Guru, he renounced his personal self and personal identity, but mingled with the Guru. He would be addressed by the devotees too as Guru Nanak. This has been the glory of Guru *parampara*. The followers of Sri Chand, however did not immediately come under the leadership of Guru Angad. For sometime, they formed a separate group calling themselves Udasis, meaning mendicants one who had renounced everything and indifferent to worldly things. Since Sri Chand was a mendicant, Udasi followers preferred to be known after him as Udasis.

Angad was a great organiser. During the thirteen years of his leadership (1539 AD- 1552 AD) Guru Angad laid the foundation of the Sikh religion firmly. He was a saint with vision and dynamic vigour. A person of great humility and intelligence he could face the Udasis tactfully and successfully avoid any clashes."In his own quiet way he filled in the brick work of the edifice whose scaffolding had been erected by Guru Nanak." As the number of disciples increased, the expenses of the Langar went up. Angad dev opened more centres and organised a regular system of collecting offerings to meet their expenses. He had copies made of Nanak's hymns and supplied one to each centre. These copies were made in a script which until then had no precise alphabet of its own. Angad took the thirtyfive letters of the acrostic composed by Nanak, selected the appropriate letters from other scripts current in northern India and called the new script Gurmukhi (from the mouth of the Guru). Indeed this was a novel way of spreading the message of the Master. "This step had far-reaching results: Angad's compilation became the nucleus of the sacred writings of the sikhs. It gave the Sikhs a new literature and language. But for Guru Angad, it would have been impossible to preserve the effortless beautiful compositions of Guru Nanak. Any organisation devoted to philosophy or God-realisation and the Sikhs at the initial stage had none. The Guru never kept any of the beautiful songs preserved. So when Angad took up the task, unconsciously he took up the most important job of the order on his own.

This was Angad's best contribution. Another important contribution of Angad was the stress laid on character building. A disciplined life was necessary for God-realisation and physical fitness was pre-requisite. So the Guru gave strict instructions to all the centres of the Sikhs to organise physical fitness drills and regular exercises to keep body and mind clean and sound. That was practised regularly and a regular cadre of workers came out of these groups who proved useful volunteers for the orders.

Like his own Guru, Angad Dev did not like to nominate his own children as his successors. Before he passed away in 1552 he installed his favourite disciple Guru Amar Das as the Third Sikh Guru. Angad did not like his son Datu to take charge of the organisation. He preferred Amar Das, an old devotee of the Guru. It was resented. As recorded in history, "Amar Das's succession was not recognised by Angad's son Datu who ejected him from Khadur and installed himself as the Third Guru. Amar Das moved to Goindwal and from Goindwal to his own village, Basarke. After some time when Datu's following dwindled, Amar Das was able to return to Goindwal and take up his ministry in earnest."

According to Sikh chronicles, on an occasion when Datu literally kicked Amar Das off his seat, the latter joined the palms of his hands and said humbly -"This must have hurt your foot." On another occasion Amar Das said - "If anyone ill treats you, bear it patiently. If you bear it three times, God will himsef fight for you the fourth time."

(Macauliffe, The Sikh Religion, Vol III, p 70)

Angad's farsightedness proved correct. An incarnation of humility and patience, as preached and practised by Guru Nanak, Angad wanted the leadership to be taken over by a person spiritually high, mentally fully perfect and normally an ideal Sikh.

Who else could it be next to him than Guru Amar Das?

6

Guru Amar Das Man of Letters and Action

Amar Das was the Third Guru and religious head of Sikhs for over twenty two years (1552-74 AD). He organised the whole order and developed the teachings of the Master. He was responsible for carrying out a number of reformations and laid the organisational foundation on a firm footing

Amar Das was mainly credited with popularising the spread of community Kitchen-Langar- already instituted by Guru Nanak. This common get together did away with caste and status consciousness among the followers of the order. Sikhism was made more popular through simple discourse and distribution of religious literature.

Guru Amar Das was born in the tiny village Basraka near Amritsar in a Bhalla family in 1479 AD. His parents hailed fom warrior race - Kshatriya. His father was Tejbhan and mother Bhakta Kaur. They were not very affluent but fairly well-to-do family.

Amar Das was married at the age of forty. His wife Manasa Devi was a devoted lady. Both Amar and Manasa used to follow the Vaishnava way of life. Amar Das had two daughters and two sons and host of relatives. They were leading quite peaceful and happy life. They were known for their affable disposition and kind demeanour. No mendicant left their door unattended. Special attention was given to Vaishnavas. The whole family was known for its charitable disposition.

From early childhood Amar Das was deeply spiritually minded. He used to lead a very abstemious life. He was extremely fond of Ganga bath and a regular worshipper of the Almighty. Amritsar was away from the sacred river but the saint would take the trouble of regularly trekking his way, on foot, to have his usual holy bath. One day, it so happened that a mendicant also joined him on return journey.

Amar Das prepared food, offered it to Vishnu, the family deity and requested the holy man to join him in his lunch. The holy man seeing his meek demeanour was very much attracted towards him. They had a common lunch. The mendicant was happy. But happier still was Amar Das as he not only served a monk but also saved him from the drudgery of cooking in the scorching heat.

This hospitality proved costly as the holy man turned hostile, the moment he came to know during post lunch conversation, that Amar Das was yet to get his initiation. There was a belief, and it is partly prevalent even now that unless one is initiated, one will not be allowed to cook food and offer it to God. In all important festivals of the Hindus, this rule is still in vogue.

The moment the mendicant came to know that Amar Das was not initiated he felt very sad to have accepted food from him. The poor man first offered it to his deity and then took Prasad. This Prasad was not pure. Amar Das had no reply.

What could he do if the Guru did not arrive and initiated him. He had never failed to offer his prayers even for a single day. The mendicant was angry. Amar could only repent. He repented not for offering food to the holyman but he was contrite because he was reminded again that he had not yet got his initiation. He was keen to get a Guru but could think of none. He was yet waiting for the propitious moment of his life.

The mendicant, however, was attracted by his humility and before leaving advised Amar Das to get initiated soon.

Amar Das was ready but where was the Guru? Where was he? When will he arrive! His mind pined for his arrival. Will he ever come?

The mendicant told him that it was not only for purification of the body and mind that one needed a Guru,but a Guru was needed to have God-realisation. A Guru is construed as a sun and one must enjoy the shower of his blessings to flourish spiritually. The flowers do not bloom without sunshine. A spiritual life never prospers without the exact pathfinder. Salvation could be assured only through a real preceptor. But the Guru must be the correct one. That is why they always depend on the Sadguru.

It was indeed a great realisation.The Sadhu had done him a great service. It was an eye opener for Amar Das. He had been walking all these years but without proper direction by a pathfinder. He did not know whether he had been on the right or wrong path. The question of salvation did not arise. It was not so easy after all.

The mind had always been clean. The heart was also devoted. The field was ready. One must sow the seed. Who would do that? Amar Das almost lost his sleep.But what coincidence! Listen,

Who was singing that song?

The song pierced into his heart and the pious man was simply overwhelmed with its melody. Every word of it, it seemed, was addressed to him! The pretty girl was still singing the song to the accompaniment of a rebeck :

> The great Almighty Lord is sitting on His throne
> just like nectar
> How to reach his feet ?
> Is it ever possible without the blessings of the Sadguru?
> Will any ferry carry (me) to the other shore?
> The palace of my Lord is bound covered by golden walls
> There are hillocks of pearls and diamonds inside
> Without the ladder of the blessings of the Guru
> How will you reach there ?
> Through the meditation of the Guru
> Go to the Lord
> Through the light of the Guru see Him
> Without the Sadguru no body else knows the real way of crossing the ferry
> You will cross the river only through the boat of the Guru

Who was singing the melodious song with a fine rebeck ? It was a heavenly melody. And how was it every word of the song seemed to be meant for Amar Das ! Somebody must have been offering here prayers. It was dawn. Amar Das was waiting for morning,the daybreak to dispel darkness of ignorance. It was from his brother's house. Only recently one of his nephews got married to the daughter of the illustrious Sikh Guru Angad Dev. She was Amro, who must have been singing the hymn.

Amar Das immediately met the girl.

"Tell me dear, 'who taught you this beautiful song? And who had composed it?"

"I learnt it from my father, Sir."

"You mean Guru Angad Dev?"

"Yes Sir. It has also been composed by him,"said the girl bashfully."

Amar Das immediately felt that some invisible force was leading him from darkness to light. He felt he had got the correct guide, the Sadguru. This must have been the hint of the mendicant. This must have been the meaning of the morning prayer song. It all signified that his preceptor was not an ordinary man. He revealed himself after throwing proper hints through the mendicant and the daughter. The mendicant insisted on a spiritual guide. The daughter repeated the same. The stirring mind would not settle down so easily. Amar Das must surrender himself at the feet of the Guru.

Along with the Saint's daughter Bibi Amro, Amar Das reached Guru Angad. The very sight of the Guru sent a vibration in his whole mind and body. Yes, this was the man of my dream. He felt he knew the Guru for ages. There was a glow on his face. Guru Angad Dev at once came and welcomed him with warm embrace. He knew very well this was the man, chosen to take over the charge of spiritual leadership of the order. He gave him final shelter at his feet. He too was equally eagerly waiting for the devoted disciple to arrive. Guru Angad whole-heartedly greeted Amar Das, the God-man chosen to be ordained as the Third Sikh Guru.

It was equally necessary for Guru Angad to prepare a successor to take charge of spiritual leadership of the whole organisation. Guru Angad realised that none of his sons was quite suited to take over the mantle of leadership. There was no one else in the order to shoulder it either. He was looking for one who had the capacity to receive the spiritual power and work as a big power house for the Truth seekers. Guru Angad was a great clairvoyant. He could immediately recognise the proper man. The humility, the seeker's eyes, the physiognomy of the newly arrived devotee showed all the signs of a future spiritual leader. A saint of perfect realised soul that Guru Angad was, he felt the future potentiality of Amar Das and at once took him to his heart as a dear one. Khadur simply fascinated Amar Das. He too felt he had reached the portals of a dear one. He was not treating himself as an outsider. It was his own house - the temple of his Lord.

Amar Das liked Khadur. There was a novelty in the new experience. All the devotees would sit together and take their food in a row. They would of course take common food. Amar Das a true Vaishnava was a strict vegetarian. That day the common kitchen served only meat and bread.

Amar Das was initially hesitant.How could he take the meal? He never touched meat in his whole life. He was hesitating to tell the Guru anything about it.

As he was thinking all these things, the all knowing Antaryami Guru sent a word to the kitchen to prepare vegetarian food for the new comer. The embarrassment of the devotee was over but a new suspicion arose in his mind. Was it an experiment with him? Did he expect me to take the common food along with all and forget about minor details of the food? Quite possibe. He thought he should have taken the common food. May be that was the Guru s intention to get him over the rituals and superstitious dogmas of religion.

He immediately informed the kitchen that he would take the common food. He would not mind taking meat. He wanted to join the fraternity fully. He wanted to identify himself fully with the order, the Guru faithfully and perfectly.

The Guru was immensely happy. He sent for him and told him, "Our tradition is to share our common food in a common row. It is immaterial whether it is vegetarian or non-vegetarian. That is not so important a matter for decision. The important matter is to decide that one must not usurp another person's wealth; another person's wife must be looked like a mother; one must not indulge in gossip about others; must avoid jealousy, greed and pride. Guru Angad finally initiated Amar Das on an auspicious day.

In no time Amar Das became a hot favourite of Guru Angad. He would shadow the Guru constantly and looked after his personal comforts. He did it because he was convinced - some of the hymns included in Adi Granth clearly expressed this - that without the blessings of the Guru none can progress even for a step in the spiritual path. Angad liked this dynamic disciple's patent humility and at the same time the warmth of his enthusiasm. The new comer was ready every moment for an order and if it did not come from him he would himself suggest plan and with the sanction of the preceptor would start the work. He had tremendous capacity - physical, mental and intellectual - a rare thing for any God-man. He was a very simple and sincere man, honest to the core. He was an ideal disciple and more than that an ideal preceptor.

Guru Angad trained Amar Das as an all round spiritual leader. From Guru Angad he learnt that ego and personal vanity were to be removed only through a spirit of service to man and only through that service can salvation be achieved. Amar Das by dint of his personal achievement, made himself popular to one and all.

There was one devotee of the order, Govinda by name. He had a family dispute. He was a well-to-do person. He promised to build a colony for Sikhs after winning his case. He wanted to take Guru Angad to sanctify the place because the whole day's work was being demolished at night by some unknown hand regularly.

The Guru prophesied that this colony would one day be a centre of prayer by the Sikhs. The work was not to be disturbed.

Amar Das was deputed to represent the Guru. He would go to the site of construction and stay with Govinda. All were stunned. Amar Das, the newly arrived one? The Guru by now started reposing so much faith in him.

The Guru gave him a stick, studded with silver cap and said, "from today this will protect you from all evil. This will give you strength in all your works. Go and see that Govinda's works are completed. I wish you luck."

It was mainly through the efforts of Govinda and Amar Das that the new Sikh colony took shape. Amar Das named it as Goindwal. There was no difficulty. Both came to Guru Angad and pleaded him to come and stay at the new township and sanctify it by making it the headquarters.

The Guru did not agree to shift to the new township."I cannot leave Khadur. Govinda, I understand your sentiments. You want me near you, but it is not possible.But do not lose heart. I am deputing Amar Das who will stay there with you permanently. You will see gradually this township will turn into a central place for the pilgrims and will spread the message of Guru Nanak to millions from there.

Amar Das could not control his tears. He wanted to serve the Guru and stay near him. But the task has already been assigned to him and he must carry that out without any protest.

Guru Angad realised his feeling. He told Amar Das, " I understand your difficulties. I appreciate your sentiments. You may do one thing. You may live at both Khadur and Goindwal. During the day you will stay with me and look after me. At night you will stay at Goindwal. It will be a nice experiment. Of course, you will have to run a lot."

Amar Das felt delighted. He was not afraid of running to and fro. He was more than satisfied that the Guru acceded to his desire and gave him the chance to serve him personally. He was prepared to do anything if it satisfied the Guru. At night Amar Das would spend the whole time in Bhajan and meditation at Goindwal. He would take regular classes with the devotees there. At dawn he would reach Khadur. Macauliffe had described the daily routine of this great devotee.

Amar das was an old devotee, almost on the verge of old age. At this time a beaming glow used to shine on his face. He would be completely lost in devotion and self-sacrifice. He would get up at dawn, an hour before morning at Goindwal. With Bhajans on his lips he would rush to the sacred river Vyas.Therefrom he would carry a big bucket of water for the bath of the Guru. Then he would rush to Khadur. By the time he was half way through, the recitation of hymns from Japji would have been over. He would give a bath to the Guru and listen to the holy Asha Ki Var.

Then Amar Das would be busy with the huge kitchen work. He would carry water from well, collect wood for fuel from forest, and clean the utensils.

In the evening he would be busy in religious discourses and listen to Sodai. Then would start the evening prayer. Then he would serve the Guru. He would give him a massage, feed him and would wait till he want to sleep. Then only he would return to Goindwal on foot. On his way he would recite hymns composed by Nanak, Angad or himself. Not a single moment was wasted. Not a minute was spent in rest.

The spot where the Guru would finish the recitation of Japji every day before dawn has been reverentially called Damdama,the breathing spot. It was here that the Guru had a moment's breathing time. It is a sacred place of pilgrimage even today. A temple has been erected there. And many pilgrims touch it to pay their tribute to the great Guru.

Gradually Goindwal became a great centre of the Sikhs. The popular teachings of the saint, his direct approach in a very simple style attracted thousands to listen to the message of Nanak. Thousands joined the order and followed the teachings of Guru Amar Das. The saint left his home town and finally settled at Goindwal which he literally built brick by brick physically and spiritually.

Tapa was a wayfare mendicant who was terribly jealous of Guru Angad's popularity. Once there was a drought in Punjab, resulting in death of men and animals. This self-styled saint portended that the calamity came because of Guru Angad. Once he left Khadur, everything would be alright. The unlettered inhabitants approached the saint and told him everything. Without any protest or any argument the saint left Khadur in the interest of the people. He did not listen to the arguments of his close followers like Bhai Buddha. The saint pacified him by quoting from Guru Nanak's message of tolerance, patience and humility. One must pardon the sinners said the greatest of the Gurus. He took shelter in a forest nearby.

Amar Das knew nothing of the whole affair. When he reached Khadur from Goindwal, as usual, he found the idol of his heart missing. He got furious. He told the unlettered inhabitants to get the Guru back. Meanwhile Tapa could not get any rains through his spiritual power.How could the poor man? If he had any spiritual power he would have first got rid of his jealousy. The angry crowd turned Tapa out of the village after giving him a thorough thrashing. They left for the forest to get Angad back home. Angad was angry with Amar Das. Even my constant company could not give you the proper training. "It seems I have failed to convey to you the real message of the Master."

Amar Das saw the real self of the Guru, an incarnation of compassion, kindness, symbol of peace and idol of tolerance and serene beauty. He felt sad at his own behaviour andfell at the feet of the Guru.

"You have seen pearls and diamonds. They are so small to see but how precious they are because of their inner brightness and purity. It is only through humility that one gets real knowledge. That needs patience. A small seed has to hide in darkness under earth only then it turns a sapling and finally sprouts into a huge tree. Humility is the key to success."

Amar Das had the lesson of his life. He was never seen losing his patience,temperonanybody inthe rest of his life. Amar Das succeeded in persuading the Guru to return to Khadur. He was the happiest man.

On their way the party stopped for a while at Bhoiro. Angad's disciple Khioyan was living there. He immediately rushed there to welcome the guests. All were happily received and fed well. Suddenly Amar Das went into a trance and said, "I feel sad that our fellow disciple Khioyan has no son. I bless him so that God grant him a son."

How could Amar Das have this audacity of showering his blessings to another fellow disciple when Guru Angad was also standing there ?

All were surprised. How was that? It was normally against normal demeanour to bless anybody in the presence of the Guru. The fellow disciples did not approve this spontaneous blessings by Amar Das. They thought perhaps Amar Das was aspiring to take spiritual leadership from Guru Angad. Perhaps he was preparing himself for that. Somebody else thought perhaps this was a trick to come into prominence.

Guru Angad understood the whole thing and came to Amar Das's rescue. He felt that Amar Das did not do it on his own. At that moment the spiritual power was transmitted to him and this was the effect.

"From now this will happen with Amar Das. He is the one who is getting this message transmitted to him because of constant meditation on me and the Great Guru Nanak."

Amar Das felt absolutely flabbergasted when he came to his

normal senses. What had hppened to him ? "You will see, soon Amar Das will give lead to thousands of spiritually hungry men and women. All the signs of greatness are there. His eyes are so serene, he looks only at his Guru (he did not care for anything else). The two hands are always busy serving the Guru. His feet are blessed because he is always busy serving the Guru. His feet are blessed because he always goes to see great saints on foot, his ears are blessed because he listens only to divine songs. His tongue is blessed because all the time he is uttering the holy name of Guru Nanak." No disciple had ever the good opportunity to get such appreciation from the preceptor in the presence of all devotees. This was perhaps done spontaneously by the Guru to convince the followers of the spiritual attainment of Amar Das to whom he felt like leaving the whole leadership.

Guru Angad occasionally showed Amar Das his affection by showering him special honour on him. That was the reason of heart burning for many. The saint paid no heed to that. He served his Guru with single hearted devotion and his only ambition was to serve him. He wanted nothing in return.He was without any desire, a person who had complete control over himself and always devoted either to duty to the preceptor, or absorbed in deep meditation.

Long before his declaration in public, Guru Angad more or less had decided long back about the successor issue. He had decided to assign the responsibility to Amar Das though he kept it a secret, he prepared Amar Das for it step by step intellectually, spiritually. He transmitted finally all his spiritual powers to Amar Das although he knew that the followers had their eyes on some more senior persons which included his own two sons.

Amar Das never forgot the incident of his first day at the Langar. That was the first eye opener in his life. It would be interesting to note it was left to this very saint to popularise the community lunch as part of the organisation. To quote Khushwant Singh,"He (Guru Amar Das) made Langar an integral institution of the Sikh church by insisting that any one who wanted to see him had first to accept his hospitality by eating with the disciples."

(A History of the Sikhs,pp 52-53)

His motto was 'pehle pangat piche sangat' - First sit in a row in the kitchen,then seek the company of the Guru.' Amar Das was an extremely popular Guru. We are told "The number of the Guru's visitors increased so much that Goindwal, where he lived, grew from an insignificant hamlet to a sizeable town. Among the people who visited him was Emperor Akbar, who was so impressed with the way of life at Goindwal that he assigned the revenues of several villages to the Guru's daughter,Bhani, as a marriage gift. Royal patronage gave further momentum to Nanak's movement."

This was perhaps not correct. Akbar used to visit all the contemporary saints for his personal spiritual pursuit. It has been recorded that he visited Meera also secretly. He himself had an ambition to found a religion the Din-i-Ilahi. Nanak's movement was a popular one. It was mainly the general masses who were attracted by the Guru's universality of faith. His simple way of God-realisation, opposition to caste system, the preaching of the holy name was a great attraction for all. By offering tribute to the third Guru, Akbar had elevated himself before the masses, not the great faith of the Guru. It was already high. India has a tradition where renunciation is respected above royal authority."India has had its ages of silver and gold but the highest honour has always been reserved for the sage and the ascetic rather than for the king. And even among temporal rulers, those who exemplified wisdom and obedience to Dharma have ranked above mere warriors. Renunciation and not acquisition, restraint not indulgence, is the essence of Indian culture."

It was under Amar Das that the Sikh faith flourished. As a practical leader, the Guru felt that it was not possible for one spiritual leader to guide the whole lot. Thousands thronged the holy man to hear his new message of love. So he had to increase the number of organisational parishes to twenty two. Representatives with full knowledge of the preaching of Guru Nanak were appointed to conduct prayers. They were authorised to accept donations to run the langar and the Gurdwaras.

The langars were ably run and could feed thousands of hungry devotees - both physically and spiritually. That was a key to his success. That was how he laid the first brick of the world wide edifice of Sikhism and the Gurdwaras—the prayer halls. Today there is no part of the world where there is no Gurdwaras.

Guru Amar Das was a man of letters. Guru Angad started copying the songs by Guru Nanak and sent them to the prayer halls of the Sikhs - the Gurdwaras. The Third Guru started organising the same in a big way. Khushwant Singh tells us,"He had more copies made of the hymns of Nanak and Angad had added to them his own compositions and those of the Hindu Bhaktas whose teachings were in conformity with those of Nanak. Since this anthology was in Punjabi, it gained enormous popularity among the masses, who did not understand either the Sanskrit texts of the Hindus or the Arabic of the Muslims. It reduced the importance of the Brahmin priests, who had maintained a strict monopoly over the knowledge of the sacred texts, and that of the mullahs, who alone could interpret the Koran."

(Ibid p 53)

Nanak, Angad and Amar Das brought religion and God-realisation to the door step of the less lettered who so long had no access to the holy scriptures. The rituals were brushed aside and new emphasis was laid on devotion and complete surrender to God, purity of mind and body and demeanour. A touch of humility was necessary and the general masses saw a new hope of better lives. That was an added factor for the great popularity of the new faith, and Hindus and Muslims were attracted to it in thousands.

It has been recorded that "During one of his journeys Amar Das was asked why he had given up Sanskrit, which was language of the Gods, and taken to writing in a rustic tongue like Punjabi. He replied, "It rains on the earth even though the earth has water in the well, thereby meaning that Sanskrit was like water in a well which had to be drawn out and could benefit only a few people, whereas Punjabi was like rain which fell over all the land."

A new language and literature Gurmukhi or Punjabi was born and nourished by the saints and as an easy medium of communicaton it played an important role in the moral upliftment of millions of people. It served more than as a literary treasure. The whole of Punjab was literally stormed by the new movement. It had a hadicap too, the noble thoughts of the great Saint being restricted only to Gurmukhi speaking area. This should have been an all

India religion. With its universal appeal and all humanistic touches, the religion of Nanak today claims followers the world over but the impact would have been even greater if, the original messages were made available in other Indian languages. True, Adi Granth consists of writings from other saints with similar thought and is a masterpiece on contemporary thoughts of spiritual pathfinders, the great Guru no longer restricted only to the Sikhs alone. He is one of the builders of modern India and his contribution to cultural history of India stands unique.

Amar Das himself was a prolific writer. Nine hundred and seven hymns of Aamar Das are incorporated in the Adi Granth.

Through all these hymns the devoted Guru praised Guru Nanak and preached the message of Love. He identified himself completely with Guru Nanak and even signed after every hymn as 'Nanak'. In almost all the hymns, the central point has been the glory of the Holy Name of the Almighty.

In one song Manmukh Lok Samjhaviai Kadon Samjhaya Jae

Amar Das Says :

If you preach to the wicked
can you turn them from their wicked ways?
They will not mingle with the good however much you try
But will tread their own wayward paths
For such is their dessert
There are two ways
Love of the Lord and love of gold.
By His ordinance alone one finds the right path.
The good conquer their sinfulness,
And the touchstone of the Guru's word
Declares them pure.
It is with the mind we must battle.
with the mind we must come to terms
And with the mind make peace.
The mind gets what it wills
By the power of Truth and love of the Word.
Drink deep of the nectar that is the Name
And let your deeds be righteous
If your battles are not with your own mind

But with others
You will have wasted your life.
The wicked surrender to their wilful minds
Their ways are false, their reward evil
The good win their battles over their minds
For they have their thoughts fixed on God.
Nanak says : The good through Truth attain Salvation
The wicked escape not the cycle of birth and death

In another hymn Amar Das describing Maya said the only true thing in life would be God-realisation. It is also a famous song included in the Adi Granth. It starts with Maya Kisi No Akhiai, Kya Maya Karam Kamae

The saint says :

What is maya? What acts spring from it?
The snare of joy and sorrow in which our lives are caught,
The thought of self that moves us to action.
Without the word there is no wisdom,
Nothing to tear apart maya's veil of illusion
Nothing to exorcise the ego.
Without love you cannot be a devotee,
Without the word, you will find no rest.
It is the word alone that conquers self
And destroys illusion.
The pious receive the gift of the Name
By gentle ways and good conduct.

Without the Guru one cannot tell
The good from the bad.
Without goodness, prayer has no meaning.
If God is in the heart
He can be met face to face.
He comes as gently as comes sleep.
O Nanak, raise your voice in praise of the Guru
By His grace you shall attain salvation.

In the Third Guru's writings we find deep touch of personal communication. His approach was practical and easy to follow. Amar Das noted, "Do good to others by giving good advice, by setting a good example and by always having the welfare of mankind in your heart." The message is universal.

In another hymn, Amar Das described the prize given to the follower of true path. In this famous hymn Ka Jal Phul Tambal Ras, also included in the sacred Adi Granth, Amar Das observed:

She put black in her eyes, flowers in her hair.
With betel leaves sweetened her breath and her lips stained,
But the Lord came not to her bed
All her adornments were in vain.
Woman and man who just live together,
Speak not of them as truly wed
When in two bodies a single light burns,
then are man and woman truly wed.

Without the fear of the Lord
One cannot be a true devotee
For one has no love of the Name
Love is born on meeting the true Guru.
Fear and love together give the proper hue
They kill the hunger of the ego
And with his name body and soul imbue
Body and Soul thus cleaned made of beauty rare
Give to the Lord, the Destroyer of Evil
Both fear and love to him the Lord does give
Who in this world do truthfully live.

The most sacred book of the Sikhs is the Adi Granth. It is respectfully described as the Granth Sahib. Although it was compiled by the fifth Guru Arjun Dev at Amritsar, this was made possible only because of the untiring efforts of the Third Guru, Amar Das. Guru Angad had started circulating the hymns of Guru Nanak to the religious centres. Guru Amar Das followed it up most vigorously. As a prolific writer he added to the treasure the maximum. Not only that, he circulated the copies of these sacred songs as he collected most of them. He had all the hymns intact with his son. Arjun Singh took up the task of compiling them. As is recorded by Khushwant Singh "He sent out scouts to locate and collect all the available texts and went personally to Mohan, the son of the third Guru, Amar Das, and persuaded him to hand over the writings of the first three Gurus which were in his possession. This process of collecting the writings of the preceding Gurus had been started by the second Guru and was followed by the third and fourth."

(A History of the Sikhs Vol. I, p 304)

Amar Das has been praised in the Adi Granth profusely. The sacred book record in a poem by Var Satta and Balwand :

"He made divine knowledge his steed
And chastity his saddle.
On the bar of truth he strung
The arrow of God's praise.
In the age of utter darkness,
He rose like the Sun
He sowed the seed of Truth
And reaped its fruit

Amar Das had terrific tenacity. His versatility was proverbial. His capacity to hard work and tolerance combined with his brilliance and farsightedness. The Guru was a rare combination of so many qualities - even one of them would have made him immortal.

Amar Das can claim immortality on the merit as a poet. He also could claim immortality as a social reformer. In the field of social reform, his greatest contribution was that he sounded the death knell to caste system by popularising the institution of Langar. It was not only a step against caste system. It was a step very much against the well established class system. By making the rich and the poor sit together, it was a novel method and deserve introduction in other societies as well.

Amar Das was not only a deeply devoted saint but also a great reformist, a poet and had proved himself an able administrator with vision and imagination. He was responsible for introducing many social reforms among the Sikhs by replacing age old traditional customs which had hardly any significance. For instance, muttering the mantras in Sanskrit without the priest's explanation was meaningless. He replaced it by introducing these mantras in Gurumukhi. Much later, Keshab Chandra Sen of the Brahmo Samaj followed this practice, by replacing the Sanskrit mantra by a local vernacular language on all sacred occasions. It was not an easy thing to oppose traditions being followed for centuries to be replaced so dramatically and suddenly. The entire credit should go to the Third Guru. As records tell "He (Guru Amar Das) sanctified a well along side the temple at Goindwal and fixed the first of the Hindu month of Baishakh, which fell late in spring, as the day for the annual gathering of Sikhs. He also introduced new forms of ceremonial for births and deaths, in which the recitation of hymns of the Gurus replaced the chanting of Sanskrit slokas. He tried to do away with the practice of Purdah (seclusion of woman), advocated monogamy, encouraged inter-caste alliances and remarriage of widows. He strictly forbade the practice of Sati - the burning of widows on the funeral pyres of their husbands."

Amar Das started everything late. He got married so late. He was initiated late. He was much older even to his Guru. And yet it was divine Providence that he lived long.

He died at the ripe old age of ninety-five and the Sikhs had the advantage of his dynamic, able and just leadership. He died in 1574 AD. Before that he nominated his son-in-law Ram Das (1534-1581 AD) as his successor. He did not, like Guru Nanak or Guru Angad, nominate any of his own sons to the high spiritual position.

7

Guru Ram Das
Builder of the Holy City

With the passing away of Guru Amar Das, the mantle of spiritual leadership of the Sikhs passed on to Guru Ram Das. Ram Das was a trusted disciple, a constant companion, thoroughly trained for the task. He was the son-in-law of Guru Amar Das.

Guru Ram Das was a great organiser. As a faithful follower of Guru Amar Das for a long time, the devoted Ram Das had thorough training in all aspects. Not only spiritually, even in the setting up the order, he was the very embodiment of patience and obedience, loyalty and perseverance.Guru Ram Das founded the city of Ramdaspur which later became the most sacred city of the Sikhs - Amritsar. Amrit means nectar. Sar is for Sarobar - lake. He started the construction of Golden Temple - of Harmandir Sahib. His public relations with the ruling Moghuls were most cordial. His contact with the royal court yielded immediate fruit.

In 1557, Ram Das obtained a grant of the site together with 500 Bighas of land from Emperor Akbar on payment of Rs. 700 to the Zamindars of Tung, who owned the land.

(Amritsar Gazetteer, 1883-1884)

Guru Ram Das was born in 1534 AD in a Sondhi Kshatriya family in Chunamandi in Lahore. His father Hari Das was a deeply religious person and mother Daya Kaur a dedicated devotee spending all her times in religious activities. As he was the first child in the family he was affectionately called Jetha which meant the eldest one. He was christened Ram Das, a devotee of Ram. The father was Hari Das, a devotee of Hari. Daya Devi was an incarnation of daya-compassion.

The child did not show interest in studies. He used to be always thoughtful and paid little attention to what was happening around him. He had a mystic mind and always would wander with monks and saints whenever he had their company. He would like to serve them and do his best to make them comfortable. The parents were much worried about the boy's future. He was not attracted to any one particular profession.

The mother would always murmur, lamenting about Jetha's career. One day Jetha thought of a ruse. He asked his mother to prepare some chholay, a popular dish taken by all in lunch or dinner or even with tea. People sold it on the streets. All, especially children and the younger ones were fond of it. He was thinking of selling it on the street. His plan was to start something like a canteen gradually. The mother was happy. She thought God had listened to her prayers. The child at least started paying some attention to worldly things. After all having a small canteen was not a bad idea and she happily endorsed the plan. She got sufficient quantity of chholay nicely prepared. With the whole 'merchandise' the mother thought of inaugurating the child's indigenous business. Jetha went by the bank of the river. It was quite a crowded place and people would gather there and the intention was to attract ready customers.

Jetha found something more attractive. He saw a number of mendicants taking their bath in the river. After their bath they were planning of taking some rest. But they were utterly exhausted coming as they were from long distances. What a nice and rare opportunity for Jetha's business! Jetha thought God must have sent him there. Where will he get so many monks together? He immediately distributed the whole food among them all and with their blessings merrily returned home.

The monk's blessings had blossomed. The budding God-man became a full-fledged saint. The mother, however became, doubly worried. She was going to lose her son. Daya Kaur was equally compassionate but one must have the means to afford it. She pretended to be angry.

Just after a few days, Jetha saw a procession of Sikhs on the main road of the town. They were all happily singing in chorus to the accompaniment of instruments. The mystic child was at once curious about the processionists. There was a stir in his mind. Where were they heading to? They were God's trusted servants and were proceeding to Goindwal to meet the Guru. Amar Das was staying in the newly set up township. They wanted to be blessed by Amar Das.

The moment one of them made a request suggesting that anybody would be welcomed, Jetha readily agreed to join them. The whole party reached Goindwal.

The Guru was sitting in the holy place - the Gurudwara. The devotees were standing in attention. With prayers in their hearts and music on their lips these devotees joined the Guru. The programme included prayer, religious songs and recitations from scripture.

Amar Das, the Guru, then started his discourse. Each of his sentence gave a direction to the young man's inquisitive mind. Jetha was experiencing an altogether new sensation. He touched the feet of Guru Amar Das with devotion. Amar Das was very much impressed with Ram Das. "Yes young man where do you come from? What are your plans"?

"I have no intention to lead the life of a householder, Sir. I just dropped in here . It was your attraction that must have brought me here.

My mind is restless. I do not know what to do or where to go. Somehow I have a feeling that you are my only saviour. Your feet are my only shelter. Kindly give me some spiritual guidance. Lead me kindly from darkness to light.

Amar Das noticed one thing. His experienced eyes could see sparks of spirituality manifested in the deep devotion and desire for God-realisation by the young man. He at once felt this young man must have been sent by the unknown hand to help him in his new task of building up the Sikh community. Amar Das recognised Jetha, recognised him as God's chosen messenger to carry out his task in this world.

He was happy. He was kind. "You seem to be restless. Do not worry. You are here. If you feel like renouncing the world, if you have come here in search of peace, you will certainly find your desire fulfilled. You will get peace of mind. Your desire to see God will also be fulfilled. But before that one must get ready to purify the heart. You have to sacrifice many things. You have to forget many luxuries in life. You have to forget your ego. You have to dedicate yourself for that through works in this temple - through service and repetition of the Holy Name. You have to serve men, you have to meditate deeply on the Supreme Being.

Guru Amar Das initiated Ram Das. It was an altogther a new life for Ram Das. The land was ready. It was fully prepared. Now the seed has been sowed.

A deeply devoted soul that Ram Das was, he soon proved to be one of the trusted disciples of the Guru. He was extremely popular as a good worker. He was equally known for his spiritual pursuits and selfless dedication. The Guru was extremely happy with his performance. In loyality and devotion, he had surpassed all.

Amar Das was very much fond of Jetha. He had a beautiful daughter called Bibi Bhani. Amar Das gave her in marriage to his most affectionate disciple Ram Das. This was a new intimate connection that the saint built up with his favourite disciple. Even after marriage, Ram Das never relaxed from his path of devotion for a single day. Ram Das always got himself engrossed in the service to the Guru and in arranging the Langar.

In his book, The Sikh Religion, Macauliffe has given a detailed description of the deep devotion and attachment that Ram Das was developing with his Guru by selfless sacrifice and hard work. The more he served the Guru, the deeper grew his attachment and devotion for him. His love for mankind - be it from any religious group or faith or any sect - became all embracing. This realisation led to creating a new consciousness in his spiritual life. The touch stone turned iron into gold just in this process. Macauliffe noted that besides his personal service for Guru Amar Das and organisatonal administration, the saint used to labour hard in digging the tank. Without paying any attention to his physical fatigue he would carry hundreds of baskets of earth from the bottom of the tank. The colleagues sometimes passed snide remarks but he paid scant attention to them. This selfless service, this rare dedication and loyalty did not go unnoticed by the Guru. The Guru realised that the disciple had dedicated his intellect and physical force to the cause of progress and welfare of the Sikh community. The period of preparation for a spiritual life was over. Guru Amar Das naturally showered his blessings on this illustrious disciple, unreservedly. With the guidance of the Guru, Ram Das attained his highest spiritual goal.

Ram Das represented the Guru at the Mughal court. When the name and fame of his Guru, Amar Das was spreading far and wide, a section of orthodox Brahmins and Kshatriyas became worried. They wanted to resist the new movement by the saint.

They contended that Amar Das was paying no heed to religious strictures and was defying the ethics of social convention by allowing people of all castes sitting together in a community lunch -Langar. He distributed food to all, irrespective of caste or creed. For this, they insisted he should be admonished. Led by one Marwah, a Kshatriya feudal lord, they made representation to the Emperor at Delhi. They pleaded for his persecution.

One senior officer in the royal court knew Amar Das. He raised objection to this petition. The emperor was reminded that he had also met Amar Das, and for running the expenses of these community kitchens - Langars - he had sanctioned some villages to the saint's daughter. Amar Das's charming personality and his deportment had won respect of the emperor. So he dismissed the petition.

But the dissidents would not leave it so easily. They came back with renewed efforts. This time their charges were different. The non-traditional and unconventional activities of Amar Das, they pointed out, led to a section of anti social elements organising themselves, causing frequent disturbances and responsible for breach of peace. They feared that one day they would organise themselves and assail the emperor himself. This would be a threat of rebellion, before it could grow further it should be uprooted thoroughly. They pleaded that his followers should be turned out of Punjab to maintain peace and order.

Summons were issued. Amar Das was to appear personally. The Emperor wanted to hear him personally. Amar Das wrote, "I have grown old. It will not be possible for me to come to Delhi. He may forgive me for this. Jetha (Ram Das), my chief disciple, will represent me in your court. He will explain the true position."

The Emperor agreed. Jetha (Ram Das) went to Delhi carrying the Guru's blessings.

Ram Das told the emperor that nobody had joined Amar Das's fold against their wish. The whole thing was voluntary. His Guru never indulged in any use of force, coercion or violence.

Ram Das made it clear that there was not a single case of conversion by force. It was the universal brotherhood of man that had attracted them all and they came to him for spiritual guidance, all on their own volition. Spreading the holy message of Guru Nanak was no crime. His liberal thoughts, his system of Langar - free kitchen - only proved that caste was no barrier to God-realisation and that it proved that all were equal in the eyes of God. They had no intention to organise any rebellion whatsoever. Their action, on the contrary, spread a feeling of equality and friendship. It was also creating a new atmosphere of God-realisation - a new window opening before all, a thing which so long had been denied to the millions. The religious activities of Guru Amar Das, by no means, were to be mistaken as any attempt to overthrow the Government, Ram Das forcefully argued.

Emperor Akbar was highly impressed by the explanation of Ram Das and he dismissed the case forthwith. After sometime, Ram Das visited, on a holy pilgrimage Kurukshetra and Hardwar. So far, nobody had heard the message of Guru Nanak in these areas. He went there with the main intention of spreading the holy message of the Master.

Amar Das initiated many to Sikhism at Kurukshetra and Thaneswar. Guru Ram Das was mainly responsible for organising the Guru's journey.

In all the detailed works of the devotee, Amar Das found in his divine instinct and farsightedness that the only person most suited to run the organisation was no other than Ram Das or Jetha.

He wished to install one of his trusted disciples on the Guru's Chair. This he must do as his last duty. It was not an ordinary chair. Guru Nanakji, Guru Angad had sanctified it earlier. He felt that it would not be possible for him to run the organisation from Goindwal. So one day he called Jetha and told him, "My son, the Emperor of Delhi has already given some village to your wife -my daughter Bibi Bhani. Please go there and build a new house and a new colony for the Sikhs around it. Let it be an ideal township for the people of the faith. Mind you when I pass away, you have to live in that new township permanently."

Jetha could not check his tears. He could never think that the Guru would ever like him to part with him like this. To Ram Das, Goindwal was the holiest pilgrimage. How could he leave that spot? And what was more painful was how he could live without the Guru? Who would look after him in his old age? And why this punishment?

The Guru could understand the feeling of Ram Das. Both had developed such understanding as they came to know each other so thoroughly well.

Guru Amar Das said with a smile, "I can tell you, in near future that neighbourhood would become the holiest of the pilgrimages of the Sikhs. Towards the east of your house you must dig a tank soon". Jetha had no other alternative. With a heavy heart he parted with Goindwal. An excellent organiser that he was, very soon he completed a small house. He dug a tank also towards the east of his house as directed by his Guru.

It was a distance of about twenty five miles from the holy citadel of the Guru.

After completing the house and digging the tank he went to Goindwal to give a detailed report. More than that he wanted to see his Guru. His heart was aching. He never had been separated from him for such a long time. The guru knew this. He knew that only Ram Das could complete the task so efficiently and so swiftly. He was immensely happy. He told Ram Das, "the tank that you have dug is on a high land. You need not dig further. It will get lively. I shower my blessings. A bath in that holy tank will earn immense spiritual power to any Sikh. I name this tank as Santok Sar. Whoever touches the water of the tank will get immense joy and limitless peace."

Some days passed. One day Guru Amar Das told Ram Das, "A little towards east of the tank some low lying land is there. There you dig a big lake. This lake, with my blessings will be the holiest spot to the Sikhs. I am giving a name to that lake in advance. It will be known as Amrit Sar."

This lake - Amrit Sarobar - and the city named after the famous lake as Amrit Sar, today has been the holiest spot not only for the Sikh but people of all religions and regions go and touch the dust of the town and drop of water of the lake in search of peace and heavenly bliss.

Guru Amar Das was getting old. He was worried over the future leadership of the community and the parish. In his heart of hearts, he had taken the decision to install Ram Das as the next Guru. But he had to do it ceremoniously and he had to do it before all. All must accept him as their Guru. Otherwise there will be dissension and tension.

But the old and young disciples of Amar Das had hints about the Guru's inclinaton. They too had high regard for Ram Das. But there were hurdles. There was Ram Dani, the eldest pet daughter of the Guru who had been married to Ram. He was the most dynamic disciple of Amar Das. He was also a dedicated Sikh. He always took maximum pains in the running of the Langar. He also took the lead in other organisational matters. In trouble and distress, he was always the first to lend his shoulder. Besides that, there was none to match his spiritual attainment. He looked after single handedly all the pilgrims who came from far away places in hundreds.

On the other hand the Guru had given his younger daughter Bhani to Ram Das, the most dedicated disciple. He was an incarnation of devotion. He always followed him like a shadow, looked after his personal comforts, was spiritually suitable for the assignment, had translated all the ideas of the Guru into practice. He had completed the new colony, constructed a new house, had dug a new tank. It was Ram Das who faced the Emperor on behalf of Guru Amar Das at the royal court in Delhi and got the case decided in favour of the Sikhs.

Both the sons-in-law were equally talented and both were equally suitable for the chair. The first son-in-law was Ram, the other Ram Das. Whom to choose? Ram was senior to Ram Das in age and much more experienced.

So Amar Das thought of a plan. He wanted to test the loyalty, patience, perseverance of both and to show the other disciples, who deserved the chair on merit.

He called both his sons-in-law one day and said that he wanted them both to construct a platform each in the Chopal. He felt like sitting on them and conduct his daily prayers. It was a new test. Neither of two knew the real motive of the Guru. So both started constructing a platform each in front of the Baoali. Both Ram and Ram Das or Jetha started the work most enthusiastically. Within a couple of days both the platforms were completed.

The Guru was standing in front of Baoali. He was minutely looking at the platform and finally told Ram, " Well, my dear Ram, you have taken much pains to complete the platform,no doubt, but honestly speaking I have no liking for it. I am afraid you have to demolish it and reconstruct the whole thing once again. Ram again started constructing the same with great zeal. He completed it again and called the Guru to check it. This time also Amar Das rejected it.

"No I am sorry this platform cannot serve my purpose."

Ram did his best. He devoted all his attention to it. And yet the Guru rejected the whole work arbitrarily.

"Yes see he is getting old. He does not have the real power of judgment". he commented before other devotees.

The Guru heard all about it. He did not say anything. He did not give his comments.

The same trial was repeated with Jetha. Once, twice, thrice, four times he had been simply asked by the Guru to demolish the platform and rebuild it.

Each time Jetha tried to fulfil the will of the Guru. He agreed with the Guru and wanted to improve upon the previous one, each time he did it ungrudgingly and with a smile.

The Guru criticised him bitterly. You are simply becoming useless. You could not understand a simple thing. I had to explain it to you several times. On all occasions you constructed a simple platform so wrongly.

Jetha kept quiet. He accepted the Guru's version as Gospel truth. The Guru could not be wrong.

The other devotees were criticising the Guru for his cruelty and "harassment"

Jetha protested. "Don't say that about the Guru. The Guru can never be wrong. Without his blessing nothing is possible and God-realisation is the last thing to achieve by the grace of the

Guru. I must have faltered. He must guide me, otherwise who would point out my mistakes?"

The Guru heard everything. He said with a smile, "Jetha, my son, you have passed all the tests. I was only checking your perseverance and patience and your loyalty and devotion to the Guru. You have succeeded in all of them. I am exceedingly happy with you. I shower my blessings on you.

The Guru called other devotees and told them all, "Look I want to pass on the repsonsibility of running the Sangat only to a person so loyal, devoted and spiritual as Jetha. His tolerance, his spirit of service and dedication is the most ideal for the entire Sikh community. The decision had by now been known to all. Besides the son-in-law, the sons too were quite dissatisfied with the decision but they had no other alternative.

Guru Amar Das was surrounded that day with thousands of devotees. It was an auspicious day. The Gurudwara was humming with sweet hymns. Suddenly Guru Amar Das declared, "Today is a very important day for the entire Sikh community. It will be an eventful day for them all." He told Bhai Ballu to lead Jetha Ram Das)to the chair of the Guru. It was the auspicious coronation of the Guru. It was an auspicious - the most eventful one in the life of Ram Das. He was "enthroned" as the Fourth Guru religiously with full ritual traditional drill. He came to occupy the rank of the earlier great saints like Guru Nanak, Guru Angad and Guru Amar Das.

For all practical purposes he became the new Nanak. The Gurus identify themselves with the great founder of the order so much that they totally renounce their physical and intellectual selves. They fully associated their thoughts, deeds and everything to the First Guru. In all their hymns, in all their communications, they signed as Nanak. This great and important feature included not only a spirit of dedication and an excellent way of giving up ego but equally importantly it added spiritual colour and strength to keep the whole community together and united.

In the traditional Hindu order, the monks follow somewhat similar way of renouncing his self. But that is only a ritual tradition. The mendicant performs a sacrificial fire where he renounces everything and gets a new life. This is popularly known as Viraja Home. This only helps in getting rid of ego.

The Sikh Guruship was something more solemn and the dedication was more thorough. It seems,only the body remains. The soul transforms into that of the great first pathfinder. Guru Nanak nominated Guru Angad. Gur Angad nominated Guru Amar Das, who in turn nominated Guru Ram Das. This may be described as handing over spiritual power and authority to the next successor. It was a novel way of transmission of spiritual powers - from one Guru to the other.

The spiritual authority was transmitted to the next successor principally on two testing methods - power of organisation and spiritual attainment.

Power of organisation needed so many qualities like patience, perseverance, tenacity for hard work, loyalty to the order, spirit of comradeship, quality of leadership. Spiritual attainment, the second requirement must be equally high.

One special feature of the teachings of the great Gurus had been emphasis on hard work. Guru Nanak was among the first to emphasise on the idea of earning one's own bread. Every Sikh must earn his own bread. This great practical message inspired the believers of the faith to stand on their own legs. For the poorest the Langar is a quiet shelter at the feet of the Guru.

Khushwant Singh has recorded that "When he (Ram Das) became Guru, he moved from Goindwal to the neighbourhood of the tank (which he had got dug at the site granted to his wife by Emperor Akbar) and started building a town around it. The town, which was destined to become the religious capital of the Sikhs, came to be known after him as Guru ka Cak, Cak Ram Das or Ram Das Pur. He invited tradesmen to set up business in the town and with revenues so obtained he was able to expand his activities to distant parts of India. The most distinguished of this missionaries was Bhai Gurdas, who spent some years preaching in Agra."

(A History of the Sikhs, Vol 1, p 55)

During the short span of life, Guru Ram Das laid the foundation of the Sikh order on a stronger footing. Guru Ram Das was an enlightened saint. He must have had visions. His realised knowledge has been reflected in his description of God. In Asa he mentioned:

Thou art a river in which all beings move
There is none but Thee around them
All living things are playing within Thee.

This was also incidentally the highest thought of Vedanta. This also became the crux of Sikh religion. According to Sikhism, "the ultimate source of all that is in us is God alone. Without Him, there is no strength in us. Nobody, not even the evil man, can say that he can do anything independent of God. Everything moves within the providential domain."

"This thought of the Fourth Guru was an echo of the highest thoughts of the most sacred scripture of the Sikhs, the Japji which says :

"The fish may run against the current of the river or along with it, just as it likes, but it cannot escape the river itself. Similarly, man may run counter to what is considered good or moral but he can never escape from the pale of God's will."

Man himself is responsible for his actions. He is given free will. Guru Ram Das was also a good composer. He composed some 679 hymns but his best literary work has been Var Gauri which narrates many details about his own Guru. They are considered to be the authentic version of the incidents in the life of the Third Guru.

The Adi Granth includes 679 hymns by the illustrious Guru.

Some of them are often quoted and reflect the high moral and spiritual attainment of the Guru. In one such hymn, Ram Das says in Var Gauri;

"He who would call himself the disciple of the
Guru, the True Guru,
Should rise early, and meditate on Hari who is God
He should bathe in the Nectar Pool
And labour during the day
He should hear the words of the Guru his teacher
And repeat the names of Hari
For then will his sins be forgiven and his sufferings cease.
As the day advances, let him sing the hymns of the Guru.
And keep the Lord in his mind in all he does
He that repeats the name of Hari with every breath
And with every morsel that he eats

He is the real Sikh, him the Guru Loves
He to whom the Lord is gracious
Listens to the Guru's teaching and becomes his disciple
Nanak, your servant begs for the dust of the feet of the Sikhs.
Who worship and lead others to the path of worship.

In Dev Gandhari, the saint narrates :

What shall I do to meet my love?
O you who worship Him show the way
Let me follow your footsteps
The path that leads to Him is obedience to love's commandments,
Of treasuring them in the heart
They matter not your untidy scattered locks,
Your stout stature, your bent and ugly body,
If you find favour in His eyes
You shall be beautiful and sit beside Him
Our Lord is the one Lord
And we His consorts.
She who His beloved is
Is the best of wives
O Nanak, why need you bother yourself.
If the Lord wills, he will show the way.

This has been a typical and complete surrender of self to the Almighty. It has been experienced by all great saints of India,without complete surrender to Him, nothing is possible. God-realisation is possible only when one identifies oneself with God. Some even describe themselves as mere servants of the Master. Guru Ram Das described himself as a consort.

This idea has great similarity with the sensitive Sufi mystic saints or equally sensitive Vaishnava school, particularly of the Nimbarka or Mahaprabhu Chaitanya Order. Like a spiritual leader of the highest order, Guru Ram Das was not only an enlightened saint. It was a rare combination of an approach to spiritual life with a practical outlook combined with a vision of mysticism.

He preached Nam and Seva. By constant repetition of the Holy name, one could communicate more or less with God Himself. By this practice one always keeps before an image, a constant reminder of the Infinite which enlivens and enlightens the heart. It enkindles the already secretely preserved candle in the citadel of human heart. "This is to be done not only in solitude and alone, but also in public where worship of the Name is made more impressive by being organised in the form of congregational recitations or singing."

The next task is service. Through service one gets rid of ego, anger, greed, fight. The bud of divine manifestation gets bloomed through this unique method. Compassion has been a common feature of all religious sermons. But service with a spirit of humility is the best. "The idea of service is that it should not only be liberal, but also efficient and economical, that is, it should do greatest good with the least possible means. It should not be wasteful. For this purpose we have to organise our means. In every work of practical nature, in which more than one person is engaged, it is necessary to resort to organisation."

According to the Great Guru Nanak, "In this world the best practice is of the word. My Yoga is practised by singing Thy hymns."

According to a contemporary saint, "The only way of worship with them (the Sikhs) is that they read hymns composed by the Gurus and sing them sweetly in accompaniment with musical instruments." It would be interesting to note that in the Golden Temple, Amritsar, started by the Fourth Guru, Ram Das, "Nothing but continuous singing of hymns day and night by relays of singer is allowed."

The Gurus had been selected not only for the attainment of God-realisation, they had been rewarded for their selfless service, sacrifice and zeal, which was undying and dynamic in spreading the message of universal brotherhood of man. "Guru Nanak proclaimed the accession of Lehna as a reward for service. He had the same light, the same method; the Master merely changed his body."

> The wise being, Guru Nanak descended
> into the form of Amar Das.
>
> Thou Ram Das, art Nanak, thou art Lehna,
> thou art Amar Das

The human race comes and goes, but thou
O Arjun art over new and whole

Ram Das's loyalty to Nanak and the Sikhs is proverbial. It is said about him that "Ram Das was a man of great humility. The aged Sri Chand, son of Guru Nanak, asked him why he had such a long beard. Ram Das went down on his knees and replied: "To wipe the dust off your feet, O holy one !"

The Fourth Guru had three sons. Arjun Mal was the youngest and the most active. He trained Arjun to take up the spiritual and organisational leadership of the Sikhs. His desire was fulfilled in spite of strong opposition from Prithi Chand, the eldest son of the Guru. "When Ram Das felt his end near, he had the ageing Bhai Buddha invest Arjun Mal as the Fifth Guru.

The great saint, in his message on the auspicius occasion said, "As one lamp is lighted from another, so the Guru's spirit will pass into him and will dispel the darkness in the world."

Guru Arjun was confronted with great difficulties. He had to face all odds and hurdles caused mainly by his elder brother Prithi Chand. Bhai Guru Das and Bhai Buddha, the trusted disciples of the order, however, through their tactful handling saved the situation to a great extent. They saved the Sikhs from imminent danger of division.

That the Fourth Guru's choice did not fall on a wrong person and that he was not biased or leaning towards somebody by sheer attachment or affection was proved by the tremendous success of Guru Arjun who came out in flying colours, both as a great organiser and spiritual leader.

8

Guru Arjun Dev Compiler of Adi Granth

Youngest of the three sons, Arjun Mal was chosen by his father Guru Ram Das as successor in spite of strong opposition from his eldest son Prithi Chand.

Arjun Dev was born at Goindwal village on the Beas on Tuesday, the 7th day of the dark half of Vaishakh, Vikrami Sanvat 1620 (1563 AD). He was chosen Guru because of his genuine qualities of head and heart.

It was recorded "Though office of Guru had been made hereditary in the line of Guru Ram Das as the result of a boon granted by the third Guru, Amar Das to his daughter, the succession was decided not on 'the basis of primogeniture or even that of a son necessarily succeeded the father, but on the merits of any person in the line." Even as a child, Arjun displayed such qualities as would one day invest him with the Guruship. His elder brother, Prithi Chand, always harboured jealousy towards his brother and when Arjun Mal was actually chosen by his father to succeed him, the former began to bear open enmity. Throughout his life he conspired against him and caused much annoyance. It was loyal disciples like Bhai Buddha who stood by him firmly and helped him to tide over difficulties.

With Guru Arjun Dev assuming the mantle of leaderhsip, the Sikhs had already asserted their individuality and a definite secular turn had been given to their ambition. Firm foundations for organising the Sikh community had already been laid with the establishment of public institutions, important among them being the twentytwo bishoprics constituted under Guru Amar Das. Arjun Dev was a born poet, a practical philosopher and a powerful organiser and statesman. He took definite steps towards strengthening the organisation. One of his outstanding contribution was the compilation of the Adi Granth which supplied the core material and basic desideratum of the religion. He, along with his chief disciple, Gurdas, finalised the compilation of the scripture which had been started by the second Guru, Angad. Copies of the first three Gurus' works were obtained from Mohan, the son of the third Guru. The works of the Fourth Guru were supplied by Arjun Dev himself. Besides adding his own composition, he incorporated the writings of some celebrated Hindu and Muslim saints and also panegyrics of some poets and ministrels in praise of the different Gurus. The compilation took many years of the Guru's life and was completed on the first day of the light half of Bhadra, V.S. 1661 (August, 1604 A.D.). The Granth was installed on an auspicious day in the Hari Mandir. The first Granthi was Bhai Buddha (1518-1631 AD). For the first time a new religious high priest was created. That was the respected post of Head Granthi.

In Khushwant Singh's History of Sikhs it has been recorded, "Since communities of disciples were scattered all over Northern India it became necessary to have copies of the granth made available to them. In the very first transcription, minor changes were made by the copyists. Editions based on the transcription are consequently not the same as the original dictated by Arjun. Exactly a hundred years later, the last Guru, Govind Singh took up on himself the task to compile a final and revised version of the Adi Granth with the compositions of his father, The ninth Guru, Tegh Bahadur, inserted at the appropriate places. This compilation was lost in Vada Ghallughara of 1762. Fortunately, many copies of Guru Govind's compilation were made before the disaster. These are somewhat different from the two earlier editions. There are, therefore, three main versions (birs) of the Adi Granth-Kartarpur Vali Bir, Bhai Banno Vali Bir and Dam Dama Vali Bir."

Kartarpur Vali Bir was dictated by Guru Arjun to Bhai Gurudas. "The compilation was made to Amritsar and later removed to Kartarpur, where it has remained ever since. The opening lines of this volume are in the hand of Arjun himself. It also bears the signature of his son, the sixth Guru, Hargovind, at the end. It has several blank pages in it. According to tradition, these were left by Arjun for the compositions of his successors. The location of the blank pages does not lend support to the traditional view."

Guru Arjun had composed thousands of hymns. Two thousand two hundred and eighteen hymns form the largest single contribution in the Adi Granth.

It was under Guru Arjun Dev that "the Sikhs began to acquire wealth and power and increased their trade and political contacts with other States, within and outside India. He was the first Guru to introduce the new dress befitting the status of a Guru, who was now the secular head of the Sikhs in addition to being the spiritual leader. His spreading fame and growing power raised the envy and fear of Emperor Jahangir who began to harass the Sikhs and their Guru.

(The Cultural Heritage of India,
Vol IV, p 314)

It was a sad event in Indian Histroy that out of mere jealousy, an Emperor should have silenced a rare voice like that of the great Saint. As recorded in history "Arjun had become the most quoted poet of the Punjab. His songs were on peoples' lips and while they eagerly awaited his voice, Jahangir brutally silenced it for ever."

Guru Arjun Dev was an organiser. Khushwant Singh in his 'A History of the Sikhs' (Vo. I) has recorded, "Arjun's first task was to complete the building of a temple in Cak Ram Das." This was the new headquarters of the Sikhs. When Guru Ram Das took charge of leadership of the Sikhs he shifted the headquarters from Goindwal to the new township. This was named after him as Cak Ram Das or Ramdaspur.

Arjun Dev was by and large most liberal in his outlook and secular in thoughts. So when the plan of the new temple building was completed " he invited the Muslim divine, Mian Men of Lahore to lay the foundation stone of the Hari Mandir, the temple of God. Instead of building the shrine on a high plinth as was the Hindu custom, Arjun had it built on a level lower than the surrounding land, so that the worshippers would have to go down the steps to enter it. And unlike Hindu temples which had only one entrance, Arjun had the Hari Mandir open on all four sides. These architectural features were intended to be symbolic of the new faith, which required the lowest to go even lower and where doors were ever open to all who wished to enter."

The four doors were significant and symbolic. They represented four castes of Hindus. "The teaching is for all the four castes, the Kshatriyas, Brahmins, Shudras and Vaishyas" wrote Guru Arjun (Sahi). The temple was built with this wider outlook. Not only that, the secular thought was represented by the new architectural design which, according to scholars,was "a happy blend of the Hindu and Muslim styles."

Foreign onslaughts destroyed the temples' original features. It had to be rebuilt. The final shape, as it is seen today was given by Maharaja Ranjit Singh. It is now made of marble stones studded with pure gold. In the entrance of the central shrine it has been inscribed :

> "The Great Guru in his wisdom looked upon Maharaja Ranjit Singh as his Chief Survivor and Sikh, and in his benevolence, bestowed on him the privilege of serving the temple."

The main feature of the new abode of god was the collective efforts of the whole Sikh community instead of banking on or begging from any particular feudal lord or merchant of areas, the learned Guru directed all his disciples to contribute one tenth of their income towards the rent of the temple. This was popularly known as Dasvandh. That was in the name of the holy prophet.

> "The masands were instructed to come to Cak Ram Das every first of Baisakh to render accounts and bring with them as many Sikhs as could conveniently accompany them. In this way a Central finance pool was created for the construction of the temple as well as for starting other commercial projects. The modest town grew into the premier commercial city of the province. After the temple was completed and the tank filled with water, it was given a new name Amritsar (the pool of nectar). What Benaras (Varanasi) was to the Hindus and Mecca to the Muslims, Amritsar became to the Sikhs, their most important place of pilgrimage."

(Ibid)

Tarn Tarn, another important lake dug by him only showed his keen organisational efficiency. This sacred tank attracts thousands of pilgrims from far and near. It is believed that the water of this holy tank has medicinal power. Even lapers get cured. This may be due to mineral elements in present the holy water.

Guru Arjun Dev also completed holy tank begun by his father adding to its sanctity and splendour by building in its midst, Har-mandir or the Temple of God. The new town of Amritsar, here-tofore called Ramdaspur, grew in importance day by day, not only on account of its becoming the chief place of Sikh pilgrimage but also on account of the immigration of many Sikhs who settled there and carried on their avocations.

Guru Arjun's organising abilities attracted attention of Muslim rulers. Many false complaints were made to the Emperor from time to time but the tolerant Akbar always brushed them aside. Two important instances were there which led to the arrest and execution of Guru Arjun Dev and which also contributed, directly and indireclty, to the growth of militancy among the Sikhs and the need to organise themselves. The first was the open espousal by the Guru of the cause of Prince Khusro who had rebelled against his father, Jahangir. The other was the repeated rejection by the Guru of the offer made by Chand Sah, Diwan of Lahore, of his daughter s hand to the son of the Guru. The Diwan was greatly offended and exasperated and resolved to take revenge.

Having failed in their efforts with Akbar, the Guru's enemies succeeded as soon as Jahangir came to the throne. The Guru was summoned to Lahore and put under arrest. He was then subjected to the most barbarous tortures. He was put in a red hot cauldron with burning sand and boiling water was poured over him so that his body blistered and suppurated. For five days he bore these tortures with serene calmness and equanimity.

During one of the intermissions during torture, Arjun was allowed to wash himself in the Ravi, which ran along side the prison. On May 30, 1606 the Guru entered the stream. The impact of the cold water proved too much for his fevered body, and the current took him beyond the reach of his tormentors."

Guru Arjun Dev was on the sacred seat of Guru for twentyfive years. The "Seed sown by Nanak blossomed into its fullness."

A secular saint, Arjun invited Hindu and Muslim saints to almost all auspicious occasions. In his hymns too, he paid respect to all sects, though he did not follow their rituals:

"I do not keep the Hindu fast,
nor the Muslim Ramadan,
I serve Him alone who is my refuge.
I serve the one Master, who is also Allah.
I have broken with the Hindu and the Muslim.
I will not worship with the Hindu
nor like the Muslim go to Mecca.
I shall serve Him and no other.
I will not pray to idols nor
say to the Muslim prayer
I shall put my heart at the
feet of one supreme being.
For we are neither Hindus nor Mussalmans."

There is no doubt that Guru Arjun Dev "had brought the Hindus and Mussalmans together in creating a scripture where both were represented and in raising a temple whose foundation was laid by a Muslim and the superstructure built by Hindus and Sikhs.

Guru Arjun Dev was a gifted writer and a great poet. "His lines were resplendent with bejewelled phrases and his hymns full of haunting melody." The Guru's greatest literary piece was Sukhmani, the psalm of Peace, in which the Guru says, "Of all needs the Sovereign need is to pray to God and do a godly deed." Arjun said :

Sarb dharm men srest dharm
Hari Ka nam jap nirmal karm.

Perhaps these were the best words of the saint. This also represented the substance of the philosophy of the saint. "God's thoughts are the best moments in life. Among all the works the only work is meditation of God. There cannot be anything higher and nobler. The approach to religion is straight to the point and the direction is lucid and explicit.

God is the common father of all, "Fashioning worlds and supporting them from inside. But he is never born. He has no incarnation. He himself stands for the creative agencies, like Maya, the world and Brahma, he himself is Truth, Beauty, and the eternal yearning of the heart, after Goodness."

The Saint sang in his extraordinary melody in his ever immortal Jaitsri:

O give me, give some intelligence of my Beloved
I am bewildered at the different accounts I have
O happy wives, my companion, say something of Him,
Some say that He is altogether outside the world
Others that He is altogether contained in it.
His colour is not seen, His features cannot be made out.
O happy wives, tell me truly
He lives in everything; He dwells in every heart;
Yet He is not blended with anything;
He is separate.

These ideas represented self-realised truth. Only an enlightened sage or seer, as in ancient days could utter sentences like these; only deeply devoted saint could so confidently describe Him and ascertain truth so boldly.

There are great similarities between the ideas as expounded by Guru Arjun Dev and Vishist advaita doctrine of Ramanujacharya. Both had limitless love for the Lord. Both were convinced that He was the dearest one dwelling in the heart. Both confirmed that "He is the great. He is separate from devotee." Ramanuja said, "He has only all the highest and best quality. He is separate." Arjun Dev said the same thing, almost in a similar vein in Jaitsri."

God can be realised through deep devotion and desire to get Him. The saint, like a real pathfinder also indicated the way. In his Gauri Mala he intoned:

Without pleasing God all actions are worthless.
Repetition of Mantras, austerities, set ways
of living, or deeds of merit
leave us destitute even before our journey ends.
You won't get even half a copper for your fasts
and special programmes of life.
These things, O brother won't do there;
For the requirements of that way are quite different.

You won't get a place there for all your bathing
and washing in different places.
These means are useless; they cannot satisfy the
condition of that world.
Are you a reciter of all the four Vedas.
There is no room for you there.
With all your correct reading, if you don't
understand one thing that matters, you only
bother yourself.
I say, Nanak, if you ever yourself in action.
you will be saved.
Serve your God and remember Him.
Leaving all your pride and self."

The above give some of the spiritual glimpses of the saint's personal realisation. As pieces of literature, they rank so high. What would be more important has been the description of the self-realised truth.

There are many similarities in the ideas expressed in Gauri Mala with the famous Bhaja Govinda Strotram by Sankaracharya. There also the saint said that "Life is full of unnecessary hallucination -Maya, everything, except repetition of the Holy name of God, is useless said Guru Arjun Dev. In Bhaja Govindam Mudharmate, "Oh the unwise meditate only on the Supreme".

The state of perfection attained by the Gurus has been lucidly described in the eighth and eighteenth octavos of Guru Arjun Dev's Sukhmani. There the Guru, from his enlightened knowledge and high literary attainment, has given some of the priceless pieces in Indian philosophy and Indian literature.

Sukhmani and Asa are perhaps the best literary pieces of the great saint. They can be compared with modern Geetanjali by poet Tagore. Both reflect the highest Indian thoughts as described and recorded in Upanishads, particularly the stress on oneness of God. They both reflect the sublime thoughts of Vedanta.

In Asa, Guru Arjun Dev Said :

"God does not die, nor do I fear death.
He does not perish, nor do I grieve.
He is not poor, nor do I have hunger.

He has no pain, nor have I any trouble.
There is no destroyer except God.
Who is my life and Who gives me life.
He has no land, nor have I got any.
He has no entanglement, nor have I any care.
As He is stainless, so am I free from stain.
As He is happy, so am I always rejoicing.
He has no anxiety, nor have I any concern.
As He is not defiled, so am I not polluted.
As he has no craving, so do I could nothing
He is pure, and I too suit Him in this.
I am nothing, He alone is everything.
All around is the same He.
Nanak, the Guru has destroyed all my superstitions and defects.
And I have become uniformly one with him."

The songs are only partially expressed in vigour, in depth, particularly the inner sentiments in mere translations. These utterances in Gurmukhi resound like holy mantras and immediately have their spiritual effect and reactions in the hearts of the devotees.

The thoughts in Asa and Bhairon, particularly represent the inner current of the devotional lives in India. God is everything. The devotee is the mere Sharar anagata, the servant, the one who has taken shelter at his feet. This idea was common to all the sages and seers. Even those, who initially had different approach finally realised their initial mistake and came to accept this most enlightened and earliest path.

Guru Arjun Dev was an incarnation of complete surrender and loyal devotion to the Lord. In a special piece in Sri the saint noted :

"I love him who is the truth.
He does not die; nor is reborn to die again
I feel from him but he does not forsake one
He is in all our hearts.
He knows the sorrows of the poor.
He destroys their pain and suffering,
He upholds those who serve him.
This wondrous form is the formless one
One Guru took one to meet him O Mother

Listen, my brothers, befriend him
Shun the love that is Maya's snare
For none that love Maya are happy.
He knows all
He is the great giver.
He is serene
He is charitable
He is the true friend and helper
He is very great
He towers above all
He is limitless."

This has been one of the best pieces in Adi Granth. It gives a description of the saint's inner realisation. The poem was sanctified by the vision of the poet. The Guru himself described about the bliss of a vision on the same song 'Prit lagi tis sac sion maria na avai jae'.

One vision of him destroyed all sins and in body find tranquility with single mindedness meditate on the one and the mind's illusions will be dispelled. Arjun dev said,

He is the treasure of goodness
Ever youthful he is
And full of charity
Worship him all the time
Forget him not night or day
Those who are his chosen
Are befriended by him
I dedicate my body, soul, and my possessions,
And sacrifice my life to him.
He sees and hears all
He dwells in the recesses of our hearts
Even the ones who show him no gratitude
Are helped by him
Nanak's God is ever forgiving

In another piece, a real gem, the Guru had said that all should bank on friendship and seek shelter of God.

Arjun Dev said:

When troubles come and you have no one to turn to
When enemies are at your heels and your kinsmen

When hope is fled, all hope shattered
Let your thoughts turn to him who is your Maker
And no ill wind will harm you.

The soul stirring song starting with 'ja ko muskal at banai dhoi koi na dei' would give solace to millions. The prayer runs thus :

The master is the strength of the feeble
He does not come and go, He is forever where he is;
The Guru's words shall reveal the truth to you
When you are weak and frail,
Without clothes, without food,
When no one drops a coin in your apron
Nor gives you comfort.
When no one helps you and you succeed not in your action
Let your thoughts turn to him who is your Maker.
And your affairs will forever go well.
When cares crowd upon you
When your body is foul with disease
When you are obsessed with thoughts of your wife and your kinsmen.
Are sometimes happy and sometimes sad,
When restless and agitated you wander in all directions
Without a moment's rest, without a moment's sleep
Let your thoughts turn, to him who is your Maker
And your body and mind will forever be whole.

The songs were so personal, so absolutely true that any reader or listener will simply be overwhelmed and touched by their recitation. They were so practical with day to day life, so appealing to the heart that the voice leave its deep imprint in the mind and linger long in its recapitulation.

What is needed is devotion, complete surrender to God, full loyalty to Him. Learning, prayers, pilgrimages, all good works, holy baths, all are meaningless if the devotee does not love the Lord with all his being. These would all be in vain.

The Saint said so boldly :

Empires, Kingdoms and baronials may be yours
And the wherewithal of power and pleasure

You may own orchards, beautiful and bountiful
And have power over others without any limit
And indulge in sports and pastimes to keep yourself amused.
If your thoughts true not to Him who is your Maker
Yours will be the rebirth as a Serpent.

The Guru addressed all his disciples - rich and poor and directed them to devote their undivided attention to God. That would be the only way to salvation. Arjun Dev warned rich people and advised them to think of the Almighty in time.

You may have much wealth
Live well and have gentle ways
Love deep your mother and father, sons, brothers and friends
Own armies of footmen and archers and many to bow
to you in salutation.
Many to shout "Long may you live."
If your thoughts turn not to Him who is your Maker.
You shall surely be dragged down to hell.

In the same long hymns, Guru Arjun Dev said, exactly in the same voice as Sankaracharya had stated earlier.

Your body may be free of fever and without sores,
Your mind free of cares and afflictions,
Without ever the thoughts of death
Night and day you may enjoy yourself
And take everything as your own
Without any reserve or hesitation.
If your thoughts turn, not to Him who is your Maker
For you will be the servitude of hell's demons.
Those to whom the creator is merciful
Are given the company of holy men,
The more they love him.
He is the Lord of good and evil.
There is none other than Him.
O Nanak, only by his grace will you find Him.
The true Guru, whose Name is truth.

Some of Arjun Dev's songs directly reflected the hymns of the Vedas - as for instance 'Tun mera pita, tun hai mera mata'. As expressed in ancient scriptures, described by ancient sages, only those he cared to see the Almighty on whom he showered his blessings.

"By your grace I recognise you,
You are my support.
You are my pride
I know no others besides you
The world is but an arena for your sport."

The Guru definitely was an enlightened saint. He had many visions as he himself had described in so many hymns. "My heart has found peace and comfort by singing your praise." he proclaimed in Majh.

A very oft quoted song, 'tun per sakh teri khul' has brilliant subtle ideas. The imagination has been most fascinating. "You are the tree and the world its branch. You were unknown and you made yourself manifest. You are the ocean, you are the bubble, you are foam. There in nothing that is without you."

In almost all his songs, the Guru invoked the Lord to grant him some grace. This was the greatest sign of humility of the devotee, without which God realisation is well nigh impossible.

Nanak sang to the glory of Hari. Guru Arjun respected the same. Occasionally he also mentioned Rama, describing him as the saviour. He raised the question and himself gave the reply. In Gauri Gaureri he asked, "How does one find peace ? How to find the God, Rama. He himself gave the reply. Nanak, the servant says by killing:

Thoughts of self and emerging in Him
Is found peace, O brother of mine,
Only thus we find God who is Ram,
God's Holy Name is divine nectar.
The thirst of your soul will be quenched
Your hopes fulfilled
Your mind will cease to wander.
For nectar is the name of the Lord
And the friendship of godly men,
The healing balm of prayer is given only to him.
To whom the Lord is gracious and grants the boon
Those whose hearts echo the name of the Lord Hari

Their sorrow and pain, O Nanak are banished.
The Holy Name is the best healer.

This, in a capsule form, provides the greatest spiritual strength - the only way to God-realisation.

Recording the great organising ability of the Guru Arjun Dev, an eminent historian observed, "The fifth Guru, Arjun Mal (1581-1606 A.D.) was a man of great organising capacity. Under him the Sikh community grew in numbers and spread far and wide over the Punjab. He compiled the Adi Granth or "the First sacred Book", as the original Sikh scripture is called, by collecting select verses from the works of his four predecessors as well as from those of the Hindu and Mohammedan saints since the days of Jaidev. He did his best to consolidate the church, and the prestige and wealth of the Gurus increased considerably.

As a contemporary remarked, "The Emperor (Akbar) and Kings bow before him. Wealth ever cometh to him. His predecessors had been content with the "fluctuating voluntary offerings' of their disciples but Guru Arjun tried to organise the finances of his church by introducing the system of a more or less compulsory "Spiritual Tribute" to be collected by a band of his agents called Masands. The early Gurus were religious preachers and did not interfere in politics but Guru Arjun gave his blessing to the rebel prince Khusro. Jahangir who had probably grown suspicious of the Guru for his great wealth and influence, put him to death in 1606 on charge of treason." A peace loving community, devoted to pursuit of God-realisation, had to take to arms in self-defence. The political assassination of the Guru had been unequivocally condemned by all historians and people of all faiths.

Indian and foreign historians have without exception criticised Jahangir bitterly for this cowardly act.

Dr. R.C. Majumdar recorded in 'Advanced History of India',

"The fifth Sikh Guru, Arjun, was sentenced to death and all his property was confiscated by the emperor. Apparently the charge Against him was that he had helped the rebel prince Khusro with a sum of money and some writers believe that the Guru suffered the 'penalty for high treason and contumacy.' But Jahangir's own memoirs make it clear that the emperor was not guided by purely political considerations." The unfortunate prince whom the Guru helped was, in the words of Terry, "A gentleman of a very lovely presence and fine carriage, exceedingly beloved of the common people..... the very love and delight of them all."

(Terry, Voyage to East India, p 411)

Terry was Sir Thomas Roe's chaplain and he had met Khusro several times, and naturally himself saw the tremendous popularity of the Guru, particularly with the masses. The Guru's conduct might be attributed to his charitable and holy disposition, and need not indicate any hostile intention towards the emperor personally. The Guru himself justified his action on the grounds of dharma and gratitude for the past favour of Akbar," and not because he was in opposition to Emperor Jahangir."

The learned historian has aptly described "The execution of the Sikh divine was an impolite step on the part of Jahangir, as it estranged the Sikhs, till then a peace loving community, and turned them into foes of the Empire."

(Advanced History of India, pp 464-65)

Guru Arjun Dev was not only a "Builder of cities and a merchant-prince who brought prosperity to all communities, he was also a man maker. His poems - rather hymns, would remake any person leading to the enlightened path of God-realisation, irrespective of caste, creed, sect or status. No doubt as Khushwant Singh observed, "Arjun's blood became the seed of the Sikh church as well of the Punjab nation."

How the Sikh Gurus were secular to the core can be seen even from the event of the foundation stone ceremony of the Golden Temple, Amritsar. It was laid by a Sufi saint.

As is so well known to all, Sri Harimandir Sahib - *the Golden Temple* - at Amritsar is a symbol of the spiritual and historical traditions of the Sikhs. The foundation of the city of Amritsar was laid by the Fourth Sikh Guru Ram Das in 1577 and the holy tank was constructed simultaneously. The city was to derive its name later from this "Lake of Nectar" - *Amritsar.*

In 1588, the fifth Sikh Guru Arjun Dev got the foundation of Harimandir Sahib laid by Hazrat Mian Mir, a Sufi Muslim saint of Lahore - The construction of Harimandir Sahib was completed with devoted voluntary service, *Kar Seva*.

The Harimandir was called the *Golden Temple* when its upper part was decorated with richly embossed gold sheets during the period of Maharaja Ranjit Singh in 1803 A.D.

The temple was open on all sides symbolising that the House of God was open to all devotees, irrespective of caste, creed or status.

9

Guru Har Gobind
Lord of Spiritual and Secular Domains

The fifth Sikh Guru Arjun was tortured to death on May 30, 1606. His son Hargobind was hardly eleven at that time. The testing time brought the factions within Sikhs to close their ranks. Petty rivalries were forgotten. Sikhs became united, stronger in vigour and determination as never before. Loyal devotees—Bhai Buddha and Gurdas, crowned Hargobind as the next Guru.

As a scholar historian (Macauliffe; The Sikh Religion) described "The young Hargobind took the seat of his father with two swords girded round his waist; one to symbolise spiritual power, and the other temporal." The young Guru proclaimed, "My rosary shall be the sword belt and on my turban I shall wear emblem of royalty."

Khushwant Singh noted, "He made it known to his Sikhs that thereafter he would welcome offerings of arms and horses instead of money. He trained a body of soldiers and spent much time in martial exercise and hunting. He built a small fortress, Lohgarh, (the Castle of Steel) in Amritsar. Across the Harimandir, he built the Akal Takht (the throne of the timeless God), where instead of chanting hymns of peace, the congregation heard ballads extolling feats of heroism, and, istead of listening to religious discourses, discussed plans of military conquests." The Guru was mainly remembered for being the pioneer to give the Sikhs the touch of adventure by giving the call to arms.

The Guru was ordered to disband the army by emperor Jahangir. He got him arrested. The Guru spent a year at Gwalior prison for his father's debt to the court, the balance of fine imposed on Arjun Dev. On release he repeated his performance. By that time he had more than eight hundred horses, three hundred troops on horseback and sixty men with firearms always at his service.

Emperor Jahangir died in 1627. By that time Guru Hargobind had gained much strength, both as a spiritual guide and as a military commander. As a spiritual head he started sending preachers to different parts of Uttar Pradesh and interior of Punjab. He covered Kashmir too. The missionaries went to every nook and corner of rural areas of the three north Indian States, spreading the message of universal love as propounded by Nanak. A number of new prayer halls were completed by enthusiastic workers. The preachers brought huge number of followers.

Meanwhile, huge gifts were offered voluntarily to the Guru. One such was an estate from the Maharaja of Bilaspur.

The gift came as a boon. At the foot of the Himalayas on the bank of the river Sutlej it was an ideal place for the Guru to build up a new small township which he named as Kiratpur. It was a peaceful spot. But peace was not destined for him.

The emperor came on a hunting expedition. Near Amritsar his army had a confrontation with the followers of the Guru. The Guru was getting ready to get his daughter married. At that time the emperor's men came to arrest the Guru. The warrior-saint was away but the royal army ransacked his house and looted everything.

The gallant Sikhs fought back the mighty royal force. Guru Hargobind left the place for safety and for daughter's impending marriage retreated to an interior village. From there he went to Kiratpur and finally to the new township built by his father. This township was later on named after him as Hargobindpur.

The conflict continued. At Lahira the Sikhs inflicted a defeat on the royal force. A stronger force was rushed. So the Guru left for Bhatinda. More than one year had passed till the Guru could settle down peacefully. By this time he returned to Kartarpur. At Kartarpur a fierce battle was fought, and the Sikhs won over the royal force. The Guru's sons which included Guru Teg Bahadur participated in the fight ably and successfully. It was a constant battle with the royal forces. The saint shifted the headquarters to Kiratpur. Till his death, Guru Hargobind stayed there.

The Guru's greatest contribution to the order was to survive, boldly in spite of physical attack by royal army. He had to face royal wrath every moment and in spite of the difficult situation he kept the flag of Nanak flying. The saint built up a bank of bold and adventurous followers deeply devoted to the ideology of Nanak. They were fully prepared to sacrifice their life for the faith. The power house of this tremendous self-confidence was Hargobind who by his personal leadership inspired the whole race. It was mainly the undaunted courage and full confidence in his Guru and the order that gave him strength to survive the imperial onslaught.

The Guru gave the Sikhs a new spirit of sacrifice for one's faith. The deep rooted message had far reaching effect. Although the Guru himself nominated Har Rai as his successor, he had sowed the seed of a mighty leadership that was being reared up silently and secretly to meet the mighty challenge of the Mughuls. His second son, Teg Bahadur, who took up the spiritual leadership of the Sikhs later on became the ninth Guru.

Guru Hargobind was known as 'miri pri da malik', the lord of the spiritual and secular domains. Whereas Guru Arjun's title was merely 'Sachha Padsah', the real king, Hargobind's title was more meaningful. His abode became a mini royal palace. "He sat on a throne and held court. He went out with a royal umbrella over his head and was always accompanied by armed retainers. He sent envoys to ruling princes and received their agents in durbar where presents were exchanged."

For all practical purposes, Hargobind became not only a spiritual leader, he assumed certain amount of political authority with him. That was perhaps necessary to keep the religion alive. Just for mere survival the Guru had to take up this unique decision. Otherwise, perhaps, existence would have been impossible.

The main target was to keep the religious faith alive. It was definitely threatened to be wiped out totally from the face of earth. In this respect the contribution of Hargobind has been unparalleled. But for his bold and strategic initiative, Sikh religion would have long back been obliterated. To inspire his followers and infuse fear, in his enemies, Hargobind changed his dress completely. "He adopted the life of a soldier, wore a sword contrary to the custom of his father, maintained a retinue, and began to follow the chase."

Hargobind perhaps had no other alternative than taking to arms. The arms, he took were in the name of God. That was his way of preserving the faith of Guru Nanak. He staked his all to carry out the mission of his life. He won and lost many battles, but his final goal was achieved. He succeeded in keeping the flag of the Master Flying and that made him happy.

The impact of Guru Hargobind's actions had far reaching effect. His whole life, his self-sacrifice, dedication, spirit of tolerance, strong determination to achieve the goal served as a message to the brotherhood. It was a life worth emulating for all who wanted to reach God otherwise than through any particular path.

The spiritual activities were restricted. In comparison to his promise and capacity, its scope was restricted by sporadic conflicts with the ruling authorities. And yet Guru Hargobind carried the holy message of the Master to other states like Bengal, Assam and Uttar Pradesh. The loss to the order in particular and India in general was the absence of poetic presentations by the Guru. He could hardly find any time to leave behind any hymns, unlike his other illustrious predecessors.

Guru Hargobind gave spiritual leadership and military training to all his disciples simultaneously. He "Completed the process of change in dress and wore two swords - one denoting the spiritual authority (faquiri) and the other secular (amini). He built the first Sikh stronghold for the protection of the Sikhs and the Hindus and to his standard flocked the Sikhs. He was the first Guru to take up arms against the Moghuls." It was not an ordinary step.

Kiratpur provided a secluded as well as beautiful lovely spot for the Guru to carry on his spiritual pursuit most effectively. On the foothills of the gorgeous and lofty Himalays, the seat of so many saints who experimented with God-realisation, this picturesque spot gave Hargobind a unique opportunity to carry the message of Nanak to thousands. As a result, the number of believers in the order increased rapidly. It definitely checked the proselytizing policy of the Moghul rulers; the impact of Muslim influence was not felt for decades.

Khushwant Singh noted, "The number of Sikhs had been steadily increasing with each Guru. The change of emphasis from a peaceful propagation of the faith to the forthright declaration of the right to defend that faith by force of arms proved to be extremely popular. The Punjabis were naturally an assertive and virile race, who only needed a leader to rouse them to action. Hargobind infused in them the confidence that they could challenge the might of the Moghul Emperor. Great numbers of peasants answered the call to arms. The influx of superstition-ridden Hindus placed a heavy burden on the organising abilities of the Guru. He had to set up many more community centres and train more Masands. In the early years, this part of the work had been taken care by Bhai Buddha and Bhai Gurdas, and after the death of these men, by the Guru's son, Gurditta. Hargobind entrusted more and more duties to Gurditta, whom it appears, he was training to be the next Guru."

(Khushwant Singh : A History of the Sikhs Vol. I, p 66)

A contemporary historian has recorded "From this time the disciples of the Guru increased considerably and in this mountainous country, as far as the frontiers of Tibet and Khota, the name of the Mussalman was not heard of."

Muslims form part of Indian life and very much represent Indian culture. But forcible conversion by royal authority was something that was feared by the people. The Gurus, too, were assured of high positions and honour in Muslim courts provided they changed their faith. The ninth Guru, Teg Bahadur was assured of commutation of death sentence only if he changed his religious faith. The Guru, like a true Sikh, a leader of the Faith and a loyal successor to the seat of Nanak, did not care; he embraced death to defend his faith.

The seed of a banyan tree takes time to sprout. It takes further time to spread its branches. It has to lie low in darkness under the earth. Who knew that the silent son was preparing himself for a great task? Not even the mother of Teg Bahadur. Outwardly these people did not reveal their inner selves. They accumulated deep spiritual power as to become a store house of such strength and finally developed themselves into big power houses. They later

10

Guru Har Rai
The Conformist

After Guru Hargobind, the mantle of spiritual leadership passed on to Guru Har Rai. He was the second son of Gurditta, the saint's eldest son. Guru Hargobind was fond of Gurditta and was giving him proper guidance to take over the spiritual leadership, but most unfortunately lost him. Gurditta suddenly died prematurely in 1638.

The biggest problem that Guru Hargobind faced was the succession issue. He found it quite a difficult task to nominate his successor. The choice could have fallen on Teg Bahadur. But Teg Bahadur, the saint thought, was "too withdrawn in himself to be entrusted with the leadership of a rapidly growing community." Teg Bahadur got a chance later on and showed his mettle. He did prove his loyalty to the faith by sacrificing his life for the community. Perhaps he could do so only after deep inner enlightenment which he could gather during the years of loneliness. The other alternative was also there. Gurditta had left two sons, Dhirmal and Har Rai. Unfortunately Dhirmal turned a rebel. He openly opposed Guru Hargobind. Besides Teg bahadur, Hargobind had another son, Suraj Mal who was not at all interested in the movement.

All these forced Guru Hargobind to nominate Har Rai, the second son of Gurditta, who became the seventh Guru. By then, Guru Hargobind had left a standing army of more than two thou-

became towers of strength. Exactly that was what happened in the life of Hargobind's second son Teg Bahadur.

Hargobind's suffering, his valour, his great organising ability, his deep inner spiritual power and insight were all transmitted gradually to his son Teg Bahadur. He never opposed his father's nomination of his nephew as a Guru. He was indifferent to that high seat of power. He only concentrated on developing an inner glow. Hargobind trained him not only spiritually, he trained him also in military strategies. Both Gurditta and Teg Bahadur, as young boys, were sent to battle spots to face the royal troops. Both triumphed for all practical purposes. Guru Hargobind trained both the seventh and ninth Gurus personally. That was not an ordinary gift of the saint.

Hargobind did not lose his faith in Nanak even in the face of terrible calamities. His whole life was a saga of struggle. His days were spent in jungle, in prison cells and battlefields. He never lost balance of mind. He was an incarnation of tolerane, patience and perseverance. To add to the agony, natural calamities conspired to embitter the life already dedicated to God. He withstood them silently and patiently. The greatest tragedy was the premature death of the eldest son, Gurditta, in 1638 whom he was growing up to lead the life of a spiritual leader. He had a series of setbacks. Gurdiita died but left a son Dhirmal, arrogant and indisciplined. He stood up against Hargobind's leadership and got some unruly followers to "capture" the seat of the Guru. Out of five sons only two were alive - Surajmal and Teg Bahadur. Surajmal was not interested in any spiritual life. He was not interested in the religion. Teg Bahadur would hardly speak a word. He spent all his time in silent meditation. So finally he nominated Har Rai, younger brother of Dhirmal, to succeed him as the next Guru.

Guru Hargobind passed away in the lap of the Himalayas, on the bank of the river Sutlej at Kiratpur, now a pilgrimage to the millions, on a spring day in the month of March 1644 A.D. when nature was resplendent with multi coloured hues of flowers. He was a symbol of the faith. He was an affectionate father to those who belonged to the fraternity. He was a rare and popular spiritual path-finder. It has been recorded that the followers were so grief stricken, that two of them "threw themselves on the burning pyre."

sand. An added problem augmented his miseries. The Maharaja of Bilaspur who was friendly with the Sikhs and made a gift of land at Kiratpur suddenly fell from the grace of the Moghul rulers. In fact the Moghul rulers became openly hostile to him. This created a regular tension for Har Rai. He feared an attack on Kiratpur any moment. So he rightly decided to leave Kiratpur and shifted to adjacent Sirmoor. That was in 1645, not even one year after the assumption of leadership of the faith. He lived at Sirmoor for about thirteen years and returned to Kiratpur only in 1658.

Perhaps it was a blessing in disguise. The Guru, instead of staying in the secluded mountain lap, had gone out and contacted many personalities of eminence to whom he presented the message of his Master. He could not be present at the important sacred spots. As the History of the Sikhs records, "The absence of the Guru from the main centres of Sikhs activity (Amritsar, Goindwal, Kartarpur, Khadur and Kiratpur), the hostility of the disappointed claimants to guruship, and the general disintegration of the masand organisation, seriously prejudiced the advancement of the community. Har Rai tried to make up for this by undertaking a tour of the centres and by reorganising the mission. During his tenure of guruship some notable conversions were made among the landed families of the Punjab".

This included distinguished Phulkian families who later on founded States of Patiala, Nabha and joined his fold. Similarly "The ancestors of two other notable families, Kaittal and Begarian, whose descendants played a distinguished role in the building of Sikh power" also came in close touch with Guru Har Rai and joined his faith.

This was a significant work of the Guru in silence. Guru Har Rai had miraculous healing powers. On hearing this, Dara Shikoh, the saint prince of Delhi, eldest son of Shahjahan, approached him to cure him of some food poisoning. The Guru blessed him and got him cured in no time. The Moghul rulers were never friendly with the Sikhs. So the saint's followers asked him the reason for this uncommon gesture. The Guru's reply was indeed most graceful. He behaved like the ancient seer Vashishtha who had forgiven Vishwamitra who had killed all his sons. It has been recorded in Panth Prakash, "When asked why he had saved the life of a son of Shah Jehan who had tormented his father and grandfather, the Guru replied, "The man breaks flowers with one hand and offers them with the other, but the flowers perfume both hands alike. The one cuts the sandal tree yet, the sandal perfumes the one."

Dara Shikoh was himself a mystic saint. His Guru was Sarmad. Dara had specialised in comparative religion and got all the Upanishads translated into Persian at his initiative. He deeply believed in Hindu-Muslim unity and did some solid research in Hindu theology besides translating some of the holy scriptures. His natural aptitude towards Sufi Saints made him win the heart of Guru Har Rai. It was but natural that in the race for ascendancy for the throne of Delhi Guru Har Rai unhesitatingly sided and gave his support to the mystic prince. Unfortunately Dara lost the battle. The new emperor Aurangzeb sent for the saint and asked him to explain his conduct. The saint did not go to Delhi himself. He sent Ram Rai, his eldest son, instead.

Somehow the emperor accepted his explanation but kept the heir apparent in Delhi with the hope of having a control on the whole community through influencing the future guru.

Somehow, Hari Rai also felt that gradually the son was unnecessarily playing into the hands of the Moghul ruler. Strongly spirited as the Guru was he decided not to give any chance to Ram Rai to succeed him to the seat of Guru. "Ram Rai's sycophancy at the Moghul court turned his father's mind against him and he announced his intention of passing the guruship to his younger son, Hari Kishan. Ram Rai did his best to re-establish himself with his father and succeeded in winning over a section of the Sikhs to his side. Aurangzeb encouraged him in his pretensions to guruship and gave him land on which to built his community centre. But Har Rai's mind was made up and before he died he proclaimed the succession of his five year old son, Har Kishan."

The land that the ruler had given to Har Rai's son was modern Dehra Dun. The direct descendants of Ram Rai (Popularly known as Ram Raias) do exist. They have built quite a few Gurudwaras there.

Guru Har Rai was, by and large, a soft hearted and kind person. He was fond of hunting and was a successful hunter but he would not kill any animal. He did not allow others too to kill any animals. He would simply collect the animals in his personal zoo at Kiratpur.

Himself a sensitive saint, he would not allow any devotee to hurt anybody's feelings. He used to say "You can repair or rebuild a temple or a mosque but not a broken heart."

Har Rai believed whole-heartedly in reciting the holy messages of the Guru. To him Guru Nanak's sayings were final. Recite them even if you do not understand them in the beginning. They would reveal themselves to you at right moment. The hymns by the Guru according to him "are final words of divinity". "As the grease sticks to the pot, when it is emptied, so does the guru's word stick to the heart. Whether you comprehend or not, the word bears the seed of salvation. Perfume persists in the broken pieces even after the vase that contained it has been shattered."

One must take the holy name constantly. "Name is a term, like logos in Greek, bearing various meanings. Sometimes it is used for God Himself." "The name supports the parts and the whole of the universe." Name is immortal. Name is immaculate. Name is "Indweller of all creation and is to be sung, uttered, thought upon, served and worshipped. In most cases it means the revelation of God as found in the sacred word." The Guru connected the faith to some of the highest families and convinced them of the bliss that a person could enjoy by constantly repeating the Holy Name. This was the crux of Guru Nanak's divine message.

Guru Har Rai, it must be admitted, was definitely a peace-loving Guru who believed firmly in the message of Guru Nanak, the enlightened one. He contributed much to the spread of the faith. He shifted his headquarters along with his army, but the missionary activities went on unabated. His support to Dara was definitely a correct strategy. Dara Shikoh was not only a deeply spiritual person, but he was also the real claimant to the throne. That Aurangzeb defeated him was a mere chance. Fateh Jung, the elephant, ran almost madly and the soldiers got confused. His losing the battle was a tragedy. In the history of comparative religion, he was among the pioneers who experimented on all contemporary higher values to be instilled among all. It was, therefore, natural that being head of an important faith the Guru would give him his sincere spiritual blessing and physical and military support. It was definitely the spiritual power of the saint that made his young son Ram Rai defend the faith in the huge royal court.

(The Cultural Heritage of India, Vol. IV p. 314)

The Guru had been fighting all along his life. It was a struggle for existence, the spiritual existence. The eldest son was, for all practical purposes, a prisoner in the hands of the Emperor. A shrewd ruler, Aurengzeb was the last person to miss the opportunity of putting Ram Rai outside his control. When the ministers of the court were brainwashing the young man or provoking him to stake his claim for guruship the saint was much worried about the next successor. In spite of personal agonies and mental tension, he stepped up the missionary work of preaching the massage of God to the masses. The Cultural Heritage of India incidentally mentions however that Ram Rai was kept almost a prisoner. It records, "Har Rai, the seventh Guru (1645-61) grandson of Guru Har Gobind, entered into relations with Dara Shuko, elder brother of Aurangzeb and came into conflict with the latter who held the Guru's son Ram Rai, who had to negotiate peace, as a hostage."

(The Cultural Heritage of India, Vol. IV, p 314)

The Seventh Guru died in 1661 AD leaving behind him the successor Guru Har Kishan, a child of hardly five. He took the bold decision against the mighty ruler who had hatched the plan of putting some of his own puppets to seize the power and authority over the new rising promising Sikh community. This complete faith in the Name and the Guru gave the otherwise silent Guru a tremendous inner force which had definitely gone a long way in building up the entire Sikh community. This was the secret of his slow but steady success in the spread of the divine message of Nanak. By connecting the faith to the royalties of Patiala, Nabha and other princely states he had laid the foundation of the faith much stronger than what people had thought at first. His contribution in the background of existing circumstances to the cultural history of India had been quite significant.

11

Guru Teg Bahadur Hallowed Martyr

The eighth Guru Hari Krishan was on the Guru's seat only for a brief period. The ruling Moghul Emperor Aurangzeb was increasingly interfering with the internal problems of Sikhs. Some of his Ministers were taking extra interest in playing one leader againt another for spiritual leadership. They wanted to usurp the community leadership and bring them under the sway of the Moghul ruler by propping a puppet on the seat. They announced that Ram Rai, the elder brother of the child Guru, had staked his claim. Thereby Hari Krishan was summoned to Delhi to appear in person before the royal advisers to settle the issue.

Ram Rai was a young child. He had no idea of claiming the leadership. The whole thing smacked of being a cooked up case. Hari Krishan came to Delhi. He stayed with Raja Jai Singh at the place, where stands today the magnificent Gurdwara Bangla Sahib. It was built to commemorate the saint's stay and of his association with this place. At that time, it was a hamlet known as Raisina. Aurangzeb just kept both Hari Krishan and Ram Rai waiting and guessing. He delayed his decision. Meanwhile the Saint died of small pox.

Hari Krishan was perhaps the youngest spiritual leader in the hisotry of civilisation and culture. He ascended the seat at the age of five and was there for three years (1661-1664 A.D.).

The child Guru died but not before uttering the name of his successor. He of course avoided the name of his elder brother Ram

Rai, who was not nominated by their father Guru Har Rai and he also knew by common sense that leaving it to Ram Rai would mean leaving the whole Sikh community to the tender mercy of the bigoted Moghul Emperor Their father never welcomed Ram Rai's sycophancy at the Moghul Court. He was definitely against his spiritual leadership solely on this account.

The dying Guru nominated Teg Bahadur as his successor. He was too weak to speak. So in his statement he only said, "Baba Bakale." Teg Bahadur was the grand uncle of Guru Hari Krishan. He had almost been in the background. For long twenty years very little was known about his whereabouts.

None could think that Teg Bahadur would assume the spiritual leadership, not even the saint himself.

The most dedicated saint of India, who sacrificed his life for upholding the cause of his spiritual faith, Guru Teg Bahadur was the Ninth of the Ten Sikh Gurus. He was the youngest son of the Sixth Guru, Har Gobind. His mother's name was Nanaki.

The child was born in 1621 in a village in Amritsar, now popularly known as Guru Ka Mahal.

As a young child Teg Bahadur was devoting most of his time in silent meditation. For long, he would not speak to anybody. People had been worried about his pensive mood. Even mother Nanaki asked her husband to investigate into the cause of the unusual silence and reticence of the boy. The enlightened father could realise the reason and asked her not to worry about it. Har Gobind made it clear to his wife that the child was not an ordinary person and was preparing himself for spiritual leadership directed by divinity. He could foresee that Teg Bahadur was destined to be a Guru one day. Har Gobind could also foretell that Teg Bahadur "would prove very powerful and sacrifice himself for his religion."

Both the forecasts came to be true.

It has been recorded that "earlier at the time of his birth he had prophesied that he would beget a son (Guru Gobind Singh) who would develop a new religion and would also destroy the prevailing tyranny in the country." This prophecy came to be true.

Bakala was a little village in Punjab where the family was living after the demise of Guru Har Gobind. It was a deeply religious small family of Teg Bahadur, his mother and wife. They were spending silent days in Bakala away from the din and bustle of crowded city life. It was quietitude that always attracted the young saint and he devoted much of his time in prayer and meditation, silently.

The child Guru Hari Krishan had named Teg Bahadur's name on his death bed. Immediately after the sudden death of Guru Hari Krishan "A whole army of claimants set themselves up at Bakala and sent out masands announcing their succession. The chief contenders were Dhirmal and Ram Rai."

There is on record a legendary anecdote, associated with Teg Bahadur's succession as Guru. When the eight year old eighth Guru, Hari Krishan was about to die, he called for coin and coconut.

He took them, and not being able to move his body, waved his hand three times in the air in token of circumambulating his successor and said " Baba Bakale", i.e. his successor would be found in the village, Bakala. Though succession to Guruship had become hereditary among the Sodhi clan from the fourth Guru onwards, it was decided not according to the right to primogeniture but on the basis of the best available man. When the Sodhis of Bakala heard of the last words of the Guru HariKrishan, there arose twentytwo impostors who claimed the right to succeed him. This created confusion among the followers for a considerable time. The uncertainty was solved by a Sikh called Makkhan Shah who came from Gujarat on the Western coast with an offering of gold Muhars which he had previously vowed to make to the Guru on escaping shipwreck. He paid his respects to the twentytwo self-styled gurus making an offering of two muhars to each. He was then advised to see Teg Bahadur. On being ushered into his presence he found the Guru in deep contemplation. Falling at his feet he placed an offering of two muhars before him. Upon this Guru Teg Bahadur asked, " How now O Sikh, you are trying to fob the Guru off with two muhars? Where are the five hundred gold muhars you promised when your vessel was sinking ?" On hearing this the disciple was overwhelmed with joy and prostrating himself before the Guru presented him the 500 gold muhars. He then ascended a house top and waving a flag proclaimed "I have found the Guru." Thereafter the Sikhs assembled from every quarter and with all due formalities installed Teg Bahadur, then in his forty-third year, as the 9th Guru.

After his formal installation, Guru Teg Bahadur remained at Bakala imparting spiritual instruction to his followers. In Samvat 1722 (A.D. 1665) he set out on a journey, visiting Amritsar and many other places in East Punjab. In the same year he laid the foundation of the Anandpur town which later acquired historic importance as the centre of activities of the Sikhs under Guru Gobind Singh. The Guru continued his journey through several places in southern Punjab and after visiting Gaya and Banaras he reached Patna. Thereafter he accompanied the Raja of Assam who afterwards became a follower of the Guru. It was during this sojourn in the East that his illustrious son, Gobind Singh was born in A.D.1666. After a protracted stay at Patna, Guru Teg Bahadur returned to Punjab and lived at Anandpur.

The details were indeed interesting. The Guru did not leave the new township of Anandpur just on his own. He was more or less forced by circumstances to leave the peaceful abode at Anandpur. He, in fact had no immediate plan of leaving Anandpur but had to do so to save his life.

There was an attempt to get Teg Bahadur murdered by Dhirmal who was aspiring for the seat of the Guru. The conspiracy failed. The Guru left Bakala and settled at Amritsar. There too, the atmosphere was not congenial. So he left for Kiratpur and at a distance of five miles built up a new township in search of peace. So he named it Anandpur. But peace was not destined for him in his life-time.

He had to leave Anandpur and proceed to Uttar Pradesh. His follwers were also travelling with him, all along. En route, all Sikhs, received him most cordially and paid obeisance due to a spiritual leader. Finally he reached Delhi. Ram Rai, another contender for the seat of the Guru got him arrested through his friends at the Moghul Court. But he was exonerated of the charges of being an 'impostor'. According to Forster, Teg Bahadur was released at the intervention of the Maharaja of Jaipur. Thereafter, he made a long trip covering Agra, Allahabad, Varanasi, Gaya and finally reached Patna. He left his wife at Patna making all arrangements for her confinement there. It was at Patna that his son, the last and illustrious of the Gurus, Gobind Singh was born.

There were quite a number of Sikh centres in undivided Bengal, particularly in Sylhet and Chittagong. When he was in Dacca, he heard the news of the birth of Gobind Singh on December 26, 1666 AD. From Bengal he went to Assam. The Guru spent three years in Assam. He just had to leave for Punjab. Everywhere people received him in thousands. His popularity and hold over local people made the authorities anxious to check his free mixing. He was again summoned to Delhi.

The summons could not be served at Anandpur. They declared him an "absconder". They however got him arrested at Agra and had him brought to Delhi. He was tried by Kazis in Delhi. He was charged for collection of money by "levying forcible exactions." In November 1675, the Guru was sentenced to death. To escape death he was given the alternative to embrace Islam. This he declined and wrote on a piece of paper which was discovered after his execution, "sir diya par sirr na diya - I gave my head but not my secret."

The execution was a pre-meditated and planned murder. The brave dedicated saint did not hesitate to sacrifice his life for the cause of his faith. This was one of the many black spots which marked Aurangzeb's role noted for his atrocities which was impelled due to orthodox and self-centred way of life followed by him.

There were conflicting versions about the course of subsequent events but the upshot was that Guru Teg Bahadur reached Delhi, was arrested as a "public enemy", tried as an "unbeliever", offered the choice of conversion to Islam and on refusal was beheaded. At the place of his execution now stands the magnificient Gurdwara Sisganj at Chandni Chowk. Faithful followers of the Guru took his head to Anandpur where they got it cremated with reverence. His holy body was removed by a devotee and cremated in Delhi. A great temple of marble was erected here known as Gurdwara Rakabganj. The holy Sikh Gurudwara stands there, adjacent to Parliament House. It attracts thousands of pilgrims from far and near. Regular langars, community lunch, are held there for all. The spot where the saint laid his life is sanctified by thousands of pilgrims who throng, holy Gurudwara Sisganj just in front of the fountain on the main thoroughfare of Chandni Chowk, in old Delhi.

Day and night chanting of hymns from the Granth greet the visitors who come from different parts of the country. They belong to all regions and religions. They silently cover their head and pay their tribute and respects to one who did not care for his life at the call of his religion.

Guru Teg Bahadur had sown the seed of concentration on pilgrimages which was boldly reflected later in the teachings of his illustrious son Guru Gobind Singh, the last of the ten Gurus.

In Dhanasin, the saint raised a question, that perhaps struck the mind of all, his son, the most. The saint wrote:

Why dost thou got to the forest
in search of God?
He Lives in all, is yet distinct,
He abides with thee too,
As fragrance dwells in a flower
Or reflection in a mirror,
So does God dwell inside everything,
seek Him therefore in the heart.

The saint laid highest emphasis on code of conduct. Moral values also got the highest priority. As a pathfinder, he made his followers conscious of need for avoiding sins.

A devotee risked a bigger liability by committing a sin. So in a clear cut manner Teg Bahadur warned that not only consciously, but a person should beware even of an unconscious sin." Out of a total of six thousand hymns as many as one hundred and fifteen composed by Teg Bahadur are included in Granth. Guru Teg Bahadur, like his predecessors wrote some sweet devotional songs. The Holy Granth has some of the best selected ones incorporated in it. One such song is "so nar duk mai duka nahi manai" has become very popular.

The saint said.
He who in adversity grieves not
He who is without fear
He who falls not in the snare of sensuality.
who has no greed for gold knowing it is like dust.
He who does not slander people when their backs are turned.
Nor flatters them to their faces.

He who has neither gluttony in his heart
Nor vanity nor attachment with worldly things
He whom nothing moves,
Neither good fortune nor ill,
Who cares not for the world's applause,
Nor its censure,
Who ignores every wishful fantasy
And accepts what comes his way as it comes.
He whom lust cannot lure
Nor anger command,
In such a man does the Guru's grace descend
For he knows the righteous path.
O Nanak, his soul mingles with the Lord
As water mingles with water.

This reflected the highest thoughts of almost all saints belonging to different religions and different regions and who were in search of god-realisation. The poem has a universal appeal.

In another song, also incorporated in Guru Granth Sahib, quoted from Asa, Teg Bahadur wrote -

Whom shall I tell of the anguish of my heart?
Greed has me in its hold
I rush madly in the ten directions
seeking gold
I suffer much wanting life of ease
And serve all kinds of people
And like a dog go from door to door
But I have no thought of prayer
I waste my human existence
I have no shame when people laugh at me.
O Nanak, why sing you not in praise of the Lord
And rid my mind and body of impure thoughts.

The saint's agony in separation from God due to earthly temporal attractions has a universal appeal. Without a deep sense of non-attachment, without a clear mind of complete renunciation of earthly lusts and lures, it will not be possible to see God. This preparation for god-realisation would become possible only by a pathfinder who himself had already got enlightenment. In the case of the ninth Guru, it was obvious from his crystal clear writing about his personal realisation of the Almighty.

The richest tribute was paid to the saintly father by the equally illustrious son. Guru Gobind wrote on his martyred father:

"To help the saintly he went
to the utmost limit,
He gave his head but never cried in pain.
He suffered myrtyrdom for the sake
of his faith.
He lost his head but revealed
not his secret.
He disdained to perform miracles
or jugglers' tricks
for such fill men of God with shame.
He burst the bonds of mental decay
And went to the abode of God
No one hath ever performed an act
as noble as his
Teg Bahadur passed, the world was
with sorrow stricken
A wail of horror rent the earth,
A victor's welcome given by the
hosts of heaven.

12

Guru Gobind Singh Warrior Saint

The last of the ten Gurus, Guru Gobind Singh was born in 1666 at Patna (Bihar). He ascended the seat of the Guru at the young age of less than ten on the martyrdom of his father Guru Teg Bahadur at the hands of the Moghul Rulers.

History of the Sikhs records,

"Gobind Rai was only nine when his father's severed head was brought to Anandpur for cremation. The shock to the child's mind and to other members of his family need not be exaggerated. The leaders of the community were concerned about the safety of Gobind, for the possibility of his being taken to Delhi as a hostage could not be ruled out. To avoid any chances, the young Guru and his entourage were shifted from Anandpur further into the mountains at Paonta".

Gobind Singh was a good linguist. He knew Sanskrit, Persian, Hindi and Punjabi. He had training in riding, shooting and was fond of hunting.

Gobind Singh had given final shape to the Sikh philosophy. To him goes the credit of building up the mighty edifice of modern Sikhism.

For all practical purposes, Guru Gobind Singh was the founder of the Sikh religion. Undoubtedly, he was the most famous of all the Gurus after Nanak. To him goes the credit of founding the basic codes of conduct and pattern of the faith. He gave it a regular philosophy. The creation of the Khalsa was the biggest and the most important of his contributions. At Anandpur in 1699 on the occasion of Baisakhi mela, he formally founded the organisation. He instituted a baptisamal rite - the pahul, the assumption of a new name - 'Singh', the wearing of tangible symbols of membership - the kakkas - a communion with the sipping of nectar - amrit -and a managing committee - the panchayat. The Khalsa breathed a new life among the Sikhs.

A great organiser and able administrator, Guru Gobind Singh kindled in his defeated and demoralised people a longing for social freedom and political recognition. He was by far the most learned among the Sikhs of his time. He composed his autobiographical 'Vichitra Natak', Jaap of his own and Akal Ustat, an addition to the Granth Sahib and presented its final version.

He prohibited infanticide then prevailing among the Sikhs and forbade his followers from having any relations with those who killed their daughters. He was a great uplifter of the lowly and downtrodden. He abolished caste distinctions and ordered that all the four castes 'must eat as one out of the same vessel'.

Gobind Rai changed his name to Gobind Singh. It was an important decision. "He infused new life and vigour into the Sikhs by introducing the baptism of the sword and adding the suffix Singh (lion) to their names".

Each one of his step in reorganisation of the order was historic and most memorable. The great Guru "organised them (the Sikhs) into a well knit religious and social body, abolished the succession of the Gurus, and placed the Granth Sahib in the place of the Guru".The supreme sacrifice of the Guru for upholding the cause of the Sikhs has been unparalleled. Two of his sons lost their lives in the cause of the order. He himself suffered untold hardships, fighting for the cause all his life, until in the end, when he was treacherously assassinated by a Pathan at Nanded in Maharashtra.

All national poets have extolled him. These included Gurudev Rabindranath Tagore and poet Subramania Bharati. The latter composed songs in praise of the saint in Tamil.

Tagore wrote :

> I do not know
> When the time will come

for me to speak out of a full heart :
I have attined my end.
I, as the Guru, send forth my call
to all of you to come and
follow me.
May the whole country come to life
quickened by this life of mine,
and may it awake and arise.
Fear is no more,
nor doubts and vacillations.
Truth I have attained
and discovered the path.

The Tamil song, rather in the form of a poem, is equally glorious. Subramania Bharati said in his poem :

From this moment, you are one
one by birth, one in life and all it means.
Let no barriers divide you
For division is Death.
Let them who break up the Aryans
Into a thousand fragments
  do so and perish.
You belong to the dauntless race
Defenders of the Dharma, God, Freedom and Truth.
Destroyers of things, cruel and unjust
Of visage fierce, crowned in *Keshas*
Never forsaking the *Kara,* and *Kachcha*
The Kirpan and the Sword
Brothers on the common road
Fearing no price but God
Befriending Man, abhorring the Wicked
Striving that the people may reign supreme.
Spurn not Virtue, be unbending to Evil.
Praised be the land of our birth
And now, let us address ourselves
To life and to glory.

On the first of *Baisakh* in 1699 Guru Gobind Singh invited all his devoted followers to assemble at Anandpur. The *Guru* directed them to dress in a particular manner. He wrote "The Sikhs should come to me bearing long hair, once a man becomes a Sikh, he should never shave himself. He should not touch tobacco, and should receive baptism of the sword".

(Teja Singh and Gander Singh : *A short history of the Sikhs*, p.69)

A huge crowd congregated at Anandpur. "after the morning service the *Guru* appeared before the congregation, drew his sword out of its scabbard and demanded five men for sacrifice. After some trepidation one rose to offer oneself. He was taken into a tent. A little later the *Guru* reappeared in front of the throng with his sword dripping with blood and asked for another victim. In this manner five men were taken for a sacrifice into the tent. Then the *Guru* came out with the five victims (he had slaughtered goats instead) and announced that the *Panj Piyare* (five beloved ones) were to be nucleus of a new community he would raise which was to be called the *Khalsa*, or the Pure".

The names of these five dedicated loyal devotees - Daya Ram, Dhaian Das, Mokkan chand, Sahib Chand,and Himmat Rai - are repeated in the ardas at the end of every prayer*. The new order was a casteless society. The names were changed as it is normally done after Sannyas and instead of Swami and Anand as in the case of Hindu monks, the new faith went for a novel title - Singh, a lion.

Explaining the significance of three of the five symbols, 'The Cultural Heritage of India,' has recorded, "Wearing short drawers (Kach) ensures briskness of movement at times of action and serves as an easy wear at times of rest, an iron ring (Kara) on right arm as a sign of sternness and constraint, and a sword (Kirpan) by one's side as an instrument of offence and defence and as an emblem of power and dignity. The Guru presented an impressive picture

Bhai Daya Ram was from Lahore, now in Pakistan,
Bhai Dhaian Das, came from a place near Meerut in Uttar Pradesh
Bhai Mokkan Chand came from Dwaraka in Gujarat.
Bhai Sahib Singh Came from South India and Bhai Himmat Singh came from Jagannath Puri in Orissa. Castewise they represented the different segments of society - weavers, farmers, barbers and watermen. The idea was to open the gateway to God realisaltion to one and all. The Guru was one of the pioneers who ushered in classlessness and banished casteism. There cannot be a better way to bring harmony.

of a simple but disciplined soldier. He combined in him the saintliness of the old rishis with the sternness and strength of a knight. Like his predecessors he kept long hair (Kes) which all the world over has always been associated with saintliness. A comb (khanga) was a simple necessity for keeping the hair clean and tidy. "These are the forms with which the Sikhs are invested at the time of their baptism in order that they may look exactly like their master, as they are to behave exactly like him".

Five is a sacred number. The great saint selected five holy men in the Panj Piyare. The symbols given to the Sikhs were also five K's. Punjab is a holy land of five rivers. The learned saint selected five of everything. In his own words :

Pancho men nit bartat main hun
Pancho milan so piran pir.

Where there are five there I am :
When the five meet, they are the holiest of the holy.

Guru Gobind Singh said, "The single Sikh, a mere believer, is only one but when he takes, 'Guru Gobind Singh into his embrace he becomes, in the Sikh parlance, equal to one lakh and a quarter (swa lakh). His nature is so re-inforced in every way that although hundreds may fall round him, he will stand as a garrison of the Lord of hosts, a host in himself - a host of one lakh and a quarter". He will keep the Guru's flag always flying. Whenever tempted, he will ask himself 'Can I lower the flag of Guru Gobind Singh? Can I desert it? I, as Buddh Singh or Kahan Singh can fall; but can Guru Gobind Singh in me fall? And will declare 'No,never'. This feeling of incorporation with the Guru makes the Sikh strong beyond his ordinary power and in times of emergency brings him new hope and courage".

To Guru Gobind Singh goes the credit of regenerating whole of India by his unsurpassing spirit of self-confidence derived from prayer to God.

The Guru gave clear-cut guideline for the Khalsa. He wrote, "He who keeps alight the unquenchable torch of truth and never swerves from the thought of one God. He who has full love and confidence in God and does not put his faith, even by mistake, in fasting or in the graves of Muslim saints, Hindu Crematoriums or Yogi's places of Sepulchre. He who only recognised the one God

and pilgrimages. Non-destruction of life, penances or austerities. And in whose heart the light of the perfect one shines. He is to be recognised as a pure member of the Khalsa.

(Svayas, Dasham Granth)

He gave a new vigour to the whole community. The Khalsa shall rule. Their enemies will be scattered. Only they that seek refuge will be saved. This is both inspiring morally and spiritually. The Guru represented a rare combination of valour and spiritual leadership. Perhaps he was the only one of his kind with this rare combination.

The highest ideal of manhood was the goal of being a member of the Khalsa. The details had been described by the saint in his Sarb Lok. The guru had so much respect for his own creation of Khalsa that he himself looked to it "as his own ideal and master". He would pay his personal obeisance in it. "The Khalsa was thought fit enough to administer baptism of the new order even to the Guru and was consecrated as the Guru incarnate".

A novel experiment was introduced by the Guru. He asked the Panj Piyaras to initiate him. "The Guru was no longer the Khalsa". He declared in public, "Khalsa mere rup hai Khas - the Khalsa is exactly like me. It mirrors my soul".

Then the saint made a historic sermon before the assembly: "I wish you all to embrace one creed and follow one path, obliterating all difference of religion. Let the four Hindu castes who have different rules laid down for them in the Sastras, abandon them altogether and adopting the way of cooperation, mix freely with one another. Let no one deem oneself superior to another. Do not follow the old scriptures. Let none pay heed to the Ganges and other place of pilgrimages which are considered holy in the Hindu religion, or adore the Hindu deities, such as Rama, Krishna, Brahma and Durga, but all should believe in Guru Nanak and his successors. Let men of the four castes receive baptism, eat out of the same vessel and feel no disgust or contempt for one another.

[cited in: a) A History of the Sikhs - Khushwant Singh, Vol. p 85, b) Teja Singh and Gander Singh - Short History of Sikhs - p 8, and c) Macauliffe -- The Sikh Religion, V, pp 93-94]

A contemporary Parchanavis of the Mughal Darbar had noted thus: "When the Guru had thus addressed the crowd several Brahmins and Khatris stood up and said that they accepted the religion of Nanak and of the other Gurus. Others on the contrary said they would never accept any religion which was opposed to the teachings of the Vedas and Sastras and that they would not renounce at the bidding of a boy the ancient faith which had descended to them from their ancestors. Thus, though several refused to accept the Guru's religion, about twenty thousand men stood up and promised to obey him as they had the fullest faith in his divine mission".

In his immortal Bichitra Natak, the saint clearly said ;
"For though my thoughts were lost in prayer
at the feet of Almighty God.
I was ordained to establish a sect and lay down its rules.
But whosoever regards me as Lord
Shall be damned and destroyed
I am - and of this let there be no doubt
I am but the slave of God as other men are,
A beholder of the wonders of creation".

God is beyond definition. In the vision of the Saint, God is described in Jap Sahib as follows :

He hath no quoit, nor mark, no colour, caste nor lineage.
No form, no complexion, outline,nor garb,
No one can describe Him in any way"

The Guru had assured in his Prem Sumarag, "If anybody wishes to see me, let him go to an assembly of Sikhs, and approach them with faith and reverence, he will surely see me amongst them".

The most important contribution of the warrior Saint was bringing equality in the ranks of all members of the faith. "All were to be equal, the lowest with the highest in race as in creed, in political rights as in religious hopes. Women were to be baptized in the same way as men and women were to enjoy the same rights. The Sarbat Khalsa or the whole people met once at the Akal Takht, Amritsar, the highest seat of Panthic authority, on the occasion of Diwali, or Baisakhi and felt that they were one. All questions affecting the welfare of the community were referred to the Sangats, which would decide them in the form of resolutions called Gurumatta. A Gurumatta (the verdict of the Guru) duly passed was supposed to have received the sanction of the Guru, and any attempt made afterwards to contravene it was taken as a sacrilegious act".

There was great originality in the philosophy of Guru Gobind Singh. He did not believe in the life of a mendicant. He strongly opposed inequality of man on the basis of caste "know all mankind as one - manas ki jat sab ek hi pahchanbo".

Although he did not believe in idolatory, he never discarded the idea of existence of God. Though opposed to ascetism, he did not deny the search for the Almighty. Man's ultimate aim, according to the warrior Saint, was God-realisation. For this he prescribed, like Guru Nanak and all the Bhakti era saints, constant repetition of the Holy name. He prescribed regular recitation of the Holy Adi Granth. Himself a great scholar poet, Gobind Singh, an incarnation of humility, did not include any of his compositions in the Guru Granth Sahib.

In Akal Ustat he wrote :

> "As sparks flying out of a flame fall back on the fire from which they rise, as dust rising from the earth falls back upon the same earth, as waves beating upon the shingle recede and in the ocean mingle, so from God comes all things and to God return when their race is run".

These were also the highest thoughts enunciated in Vedanta. Brahmanparo Brahma Habihi Brahmagriou Brahmanayahutam Brahmanay Tena gantahyam Brahmakarma Samadhina : We are all parts of the Brahman, the Almighty. We return to Him after completing His works.

Although, he did not like anybody to leave the house and join the order of Sannyas, he never dissuaded anybody from leading a holy life. In his Sabad Hazare - thousand Holy words - the saint said, a man can lead the life of a Sadhu in his own house;

> "Let thine own house be forest
> Thy heart the anchorite
> Eat little, sleep little
> Learn to love, be merciful
> be mild, be patient.

Have no lust, no wrath, greed
nor obstinacy.

In his heart of hearts, above anything else, Guru Gobind Singh was a sage like an ancient pathfinder with a modern progressive outlook. The saint gave a description of god as realised by him:

"God has no friends nor enemies.
He needs no hallelujahs nor cares about curses.
Being the first and timeless
How could He manifest Himself through these
Who are born and who die?"

Only an enlightened saint could say:

"O,Lord, these boons of thee I ask,
Let me never shun a righteous task.
Let me be fearless when I go to battle.
Give me faith that victory will be mine.
Give me power to sing Thy praise.
And when comes the time to end my life
Let me fall in mighty strife".

In the Akal Ustat the saint sang :

"Eternal God, thou art our shield
The dagger, knife,the sword we wield
To us protector there is given
The timeless, deathless, Lord of Heaven
To us all steels unvanquished might
To us all times resistless flight,
But chiefly thou, protector brave,
All steel, will shine own servant save".
(Translated by Macauliffe).

Even in the battlefield the warrior-saint relied entirely on the mercy of the Almighty. His surrender to God was total. Guru Gobind Singh believed in universal brotherhood of man and expressed the highest in some beautiful literary pieces.

In Akal Ustat, the Guru said:

"Recognise all human nature as one
All men are the same, although they appear

different under different influences.
The bright and the dark, the ugly and the beautiful,
The Hindus and the Muslims, have developed themselves
According to the fashions of different countries.
All have the same eyes, same ears, the same body
and the same build - a compound of the same four elements".

'The Cultural Heritage of India' recorded on this aspect of the Guru's teaching : "Such a teaching could not tolerate any idea of caste or untouchability. Men rose in the estimation of man. Even the grovelling slaves of the so-called higher classes came to be fired with a new hope and courage to lift themselves as equals to the rest of humanity".

The Guru assigned highest emphasis on the Holy Name. In his famous Jap he wrote, "When God became sargun or manifest, He became what is called the Name and in order to realise Himself, He made nature, wherein He has His seat and is diffused everywhere and in all directions in the form of love."

Two hundred years had passed since Guru Nanak had founded this sacred religion. Historians have rightly pointed that "The three gurus represent, as it were the three aspects of the Hindu Trinity - Nanak like Brahma, was the creator of Sikhism, Arjun like Vishnu, its preserver, and Gobind, like Shiva, the destroyer of its enemies".

These two hundred years of the new faith have two clear distinct phases.

"In the first hundred years the five Gurus pronounced the ideals of a new social order for the Punjab. The religion was to be one acceptable to both the Muslims and the Hindus; it was to be monotheistic, non-idolatrous and free of meaningless form and ritual. The social order was to embrace all the people; no class was to be beyond the pack, and though the caste system continued to count when it came to making matrimonial alliances, it was abolished in matters of social intercourse. The doors of Sikh temples were thrown open to every one and in the Guru's Langars, The Brahmin and the untouchable broke their bread as members of the same family. The code of this new order was the non-denominational anthology of hymns,the Granth its symbol, the Harimandir, an edifice whose first stone was laid by a Muslim, the rest being built by Hindus and Sikhs together".

During the first hundred years, the faith got tremendous popularity among the ordinary masses-both Hindus and Muslims, the Guru and the Granth were respected as guides to this newly awakened section of society whose eagerness for God-realisation was helped by their writings and preachings which were so lucid in style and simple in presentation. The Gurus themselves were all incarnations of humility and modesty. They never claimed any divinity. "What they wrote or spoke had a familiar ring in the people's ears. The Hindus caught the wisdom of the Vedas, of which they knew but little because of the monopoly over Sanskrit learning maintained by the Brahmins. The Muslims were reminded of the exhortations of Sufis. To both the Hindus and Muslims, the message of the Gurus came in a language they understood. Although this fact prejudiced the spreading of Sikhism to those who could not understand Punjabi within the Punjab, its appeal was irresistible. It had all the elements of a national faith and until it crystallised into a distinct sect with a political purpose, it continued to exercise the administration of all Punjabis".

The second hundred years was a period of struggle. It saw "the development of traditions which supplemented this social order. The sixth Guru was the first to appeal to arms,the tenth put the army on a regular footing. The movement also found its martyrs and heroes: " Arjun, Teg Bahadur and the sons of Gobind wore the crown of martyrdom; Hargobind and Gobind, the halo of heroism. The movement had its hard inner core consisting of nearly a hundred thousand baptised Khalsa and a much larger number of close associates among the Sahajdhari Sikhs".

Gobind Singh was a saint with deep learning, enlightenment and far- sightedness. He realised that one of the important reasons for arresting the progress of the faith was the cult of Guruship. He had analysed the past. He, too, had four sons. He could visualise the future too. Much of energy was lost in the dispute that followed after the passing away of each Guru. So he dispensed with the cult. Granth Sahib was considered by him the spiritual Guide, sufficiently rich in philosophy and literature, to guide all brothers of the faith. So he felt "The Granth could become the Spiritual Guru".

The Guru was on a military march to the South. He never

allowed any personal body-guard for himself to stop any body. It was mainly meant to extend free access to the followers and devotees." One evening two young Pathans entered his tent and finding the Guru alone, stabbed him in the abdomen. The motive for the murderer's assault was never known since the assassins were slain immediately. The Guru's wounds were stitched and it was hoped that he would recover. But the stitches burst a few days later and Gobind realised that his end was near. He assembled his followers and told them the line of Gurus was to end with him and the Sikhs were thereafter to look upon the Granth as the symbol of all the Gurus and their constant guide.

With Guru Gobind's death came an end of Gurus in person. The period of personal spiritual leadership also came to an end. The period of spiritual leadership of the ten Gurus passed on with their philosophy transmitted to the Holy Granth Sahib.

There are as many as six thousand hymns in the Final Granth Sahib. They include hymns by the first five Gurus and the ninth Guru Arjun topped the list with a contribution of 2,218 hymns. There are 974 hymns by Guru Nanak, 907 by Guru Amar Das, 699 by Guru Ram Das, 115 by Guru Teg Bahadur and 62 by Guru Angad.

After the death of Guru Gobind Singh, the Personality and the Word were separated. The Panth was invested with the personality of the Guru and the incorporated Word became Gyan (Jnan) Guru (diverse intelligence of the Guru) as knowledge. In brief the Khalsa Panth became the religious guide. This was "not in supersession of the previous Gurus, but as the authorised agency to work in their name, and it was invariably to guide itself by the teachings of the Gurus as found in the holy Granth. It is because of this that the Sikhs came to regard Guru Nanak and Guru Panth with equal respect".

EPILOGUE

I earnestly felt that it was most timely to recall the immortal messages of the Sikh Gurus who form a part of the mainstream of Indian philosophical thoughts. Their messages are of special interest today because it seems many of us have forgotten or are neglecting them. May be due to our ignorance.

The greatest and the first of these lineage was Guru Nanak Devji who as I have observed in this book cannot be called as a *Sikh* because the word means a disciple. He was the father of this great religious movment which has contributed greatly in changing the face of medieval and modern India especially in the realm of God-realistion. Guru Nanak Devji not only founded a new faith where everybody was to be treated equally, he gave the highest recognition to the dignity of man. He himself practised as he preached a strong opposition to the then and even now prevalent caste system. Even for his great social reforms, the Guru could have occupied a very high place in the history of Indian culture and civilisation.

Guru Nanak Devji in his foresight, imagination and wider vision of thought was most modern even 500 years ago. He was, like a true Prophet who could visualise events to take place. It is really a great amazement to know that the *Guru*, although never uttered a word against Brahaminism or anything against old ritualism of the orthodox school of Hindus, like the Buddha, the Enlightened one and Bhagawan Mahavira did not believe in idolatory. One must carefully notes that in our ancient scriptures like the *Vedas*, the *Upanisads, the Bhagavad Gita,* there is no mentioning of any idolatory. India in ancient days was a worshipper only of the Nature. Even today there are religious groups in India, like the Zoroastrainists who only worship Fire and other natural phenomena.

The Guru did not believe in any rituals, caste or creed and in public discarded both Hindu *Pandits* and Islamic *Molavis*. He had enlightened knowledge and in his inner vision of his lofty thought he could clearly see, rather feel or realise the great *Infinite* and the divinity as manifested in the heart of every human being. That is why he was a great propagator of equality of mankind.

Guru Nanak Devji shunned the rich who had no respect for the poor. He had miraculous power but hardly made use of them. His message was to preach love for Man and the great Almighty by uttering the Holy Name. He was a forerunner to the great *Bhakti movements* which changed the entire face of India in the realm of spiritualism.

Another very important and significant aspect of the Guru's deep faith is oneness of God. Not only that the divinity exists in all human beings, He, the great Infinite, the Almighty, prevails throughout the world. The entire universe is His creation and He pervades in everything. He is omnipresent, omniscient as much as omnipotent. If somebody cares to go deep into the philosophical thoughts of the Gurus he will easily realise and discover to his great amazement, great similarities between the thoughts of the Guru and thoughts of the ancient sages ans seers as uttered in the *Upanisads*. In my humble way I have, at length, tried to analyse this important spiritual side of the message of the great *Gurus*.

Guru Nanak Devji was a born poet and although not much lettered in the worldly sense he used to express himself spontaneously invariably by his self composed poems on the spot itself. He would even deliver his public sermons bursting into beautiful songs which he himself would sing while his constant companiion Mardana would play on the rebeck - the string instrument. The very presence or Mardana, a Muslim companion who followed him everywhere like a shadow, is also another significant reckoner to his secular thought leading to Hindu-Muslim unity without caring for compartmentalisation of anybody's religious belief.

The Guru did not certainly belong to any particular sect or religion. He belongs to the whole of mankind. I not only believe this. I do realise from my inner voice that such great pathfinders cannot be restricted to any particular sect, religion, or society. They belong to the whole of humankind.

I must record here that I wrote religiously and regularly as usual at the rate of three pages a day. This I did without fail. I have been keeping up the practice for the last twenty five years or more. In this book I have only touched how Guru Nanak Devji had influenced Gurudev Rabindranath Tagore.

The book is an honest effort to popularise and place before the public some of the basic qualities of the Sikhs. I have tried to highlight the character building programme of almost all the Gurus, their spirit of service of humanity and the hard work to which they were all used to as a matter of routine. The deep faith they had on their own Gurus' ideology was reflected in the martyrdom of Guru Teg Bahadurji who sacrificed his life but did not change his religious ideology. He preferred giving the head. His last line in life was *"Sir diya par sirr na diya"*! (I would prefer sacrificing my head, not my faith.)

I have attempted to give the details of the Sikh religion in a systematic manner by the Tenth Guru and the explanation of the concept and the signficance of the five K's - Kachcha, Kanga, Kara, Kesh and *Kirpan*.

All the Gurus insisted on serving humanity. I have also analysed in detail the institution of *Langar* or the community kitchen. The details are quite interesting for our younger generation especially. The *Panch Pyare,* the five devotees of the Guru, were also taken from five different disciplines and different States of India. This is also really interesting for the public. In fact, the word 'Khalsa' means "the pure hearted." They all promised in the presence of the Tenth Guru to shed their lives for Truth, Justice and Equality.

The greatest contribution of all the Gurus was not only in the setting up of organisation but also in the message as recorded in the *Guru Granth Sahib* through their melodious hymns. Almost all the Gurus were poets of eminence and I have tried to refer to many of them.

The secular thoughts of the Sikh Gurus will go a long way in spreading the message of equality, fraternity and secularism throughout the country.

The main source of these lofty secular thoughts of all the Sikh Gurus is derived form Japji. As a learned scholar has observed, "Japji Sahib is the spiritual message of Guru Nanak Devji. *Guru*

Granth Sahib begins with *Japji Sahib. Japji Sahib* enjoys the position of being the most pious, influential and sacred book containing the metaphysical philosophy of the Sikh faith. It is the meditation of the Supreme Being and embodies its true essence and significance and paves the way for spiritual enlightenment. It also conveys the message of universal peace, love and affection amongst people professing various faiths in the world. *Japji Sahib* explains with amazing clarity and simplicity the strange and complicated mystery of spiritual truth. It is meant not only for individual benefit but the well-being of the whole mankind. Apart from humanness, fraternity and spiritualism it also teaches national unity."